CHAOS
THEORY

finding meaning
in the madness,
one bad decision
at a time

CHAOS
THEORY

Leah McSweeney

HARPER WAVE

An Imprint of HarperCollins*Publishers*

CHAOS THEORY. Copyright © 2022 by Leah McSweeney. All rights reserved.
Printed in the United States of America. No part of this book may be used
or reproduced in any manner whatsoever without written permission
except in the case of brief quotations embodied in critical articles and
reviews. For information, address HarperCollins Publishers,
195 Broadway, New York, NY 10007.

HarperCollins books may be purchased for educational, business, or
sales promotional use. For information, please email the Special Markets
Department at SPsales@harpercollins.com.

FIRST EDITION

Designed by Bonni Leon-Berman

Library of Congress Cataloging-in-Publication Data has been applied for.

ISBN 978-0-06-314384-5

22 23 24 25 26   LSC   10 9 8 7 6 5 4 3 2 1

For my mother, Bunny—who supported me,
challenged me, and loved me through it all.

CONTENTS

CHAOS
THEORY

INTRODUCTION:
LAWS OF DISORDER

You may think my life looks like chaos. I'm not a rule follower, and to some people that looks like I'm being messy. I've always seen the world a little differently than those around me. Since the time I was a kid—whether I was walking the streets of our Chelsea neighborhood or studying at my posh private school uptown—I had a different take on what I observed. Sometimes that perspective has been the most powerful tool at my disposal, and sometimes it's been my downfall. And while I try to follow those instincts, I also need to try things on for size. Literally. I'm the kind of girl who has to put on an outfit to know if it's right for me. Even if it's an epic dress with Lil' Kim's mugshot all over it. I've lived my life the same way, trying on decisions and experiences even when the ensuing chaos felt like holy hell.

At every turn, I've bucked expectations to live by my

own rules. I've pushed back against the hopes of my parents, against the recommendations of rehab facilities and mental hospitals, against the status quo of the fashion industry, and against the limitations of my own self-worth to create a wild, unconventional, and beautiful life. Tiki torches not included!

That's not to say it's been easy. My road to success, motherhood, and my own little corner of fame (notoriety?) has been anything but a straight line. I've had my face busted in by a cop while handcuffed, sold fake drugs at a jungle rave in Puerto Rico, and gotten in my own damn way more times than I care to admit. Through the mistakes and hardships, the triumphs and failures, I've learned a little something about controlling the chaos that seems to envelop me. Now, I harness its energy to serve my needs instead of letting it rule my life.

When someone first told me about the idea of chaos theory—a mathematical theory stating that within the apparent randomness of chaotic systems there are underlying patterns that lead to a kind of organization—I thought, *Holy shit, that's me!* Listen, I'm not one to espouse mathematical theories, but what I'm learning—through trial and error—is that doing things your own way is a sort of philosophy. I am my own complex, chaotic system, with a sense of purpose and order beneath what others perceive as disorder. Maybe you can relate.

I've fought the pull of negative feedback loops, and unhealthy and downright dangerous underlying patterns. But I've finally been able to make some sense of the chaos, and that, my friends, has been key to changing everything.

For years, it felt like a struggle just to exist. I was a prisoner to substances until I finally got sober. But once I had to live in my brain without the haze of booze or drugs to ease my pain, I faced a new set of challenges with my mental health. For a long time, I was frustrated that I had to deal with these issues, and I resented the commitment and attention they required. I tried everything to feel better: meditation, twelve-step meetings, juice cleanses and vegan diets, yoga and vigorous exercise. I visited churches and gurus; I saw witches and the finest doctors in Manhattan—all of whom treated me with a cocktail of elixirs. It was practically a full-time job. I was so desperate to feel better that I looked everywhere but inside myself.

I've come to see that what makes me *me* is my strength to persevere, and to live at my fullest expression no matter the consequence. And that means I have to accept all of myself, even the parts that give me the hardest time. I understand now that my fearlessness and ability to take creative and professional risks probably originates in the same wild part of my brain that has gotten me into trouble. My spirit and my struggles are deeply intertwined, and I wouldn't want it any other way. Ultimately, I've been able to achieve everything I have in my life by being unapologetically, unrelentingly myself—which is to say, a little bit fucking crazy. Even when I got pregnant at twenty-four. Even when I almost burned down my career. Even when it almost killed me.

There have been times I've felt like a failure, but those are the moments that taught me what it takes to rebuild my life bigger and better. Like in 2017—I literally had $5,000 in my bank account, and my business, Married to the Mob, was on the verge of collapse. My brand was my baby—born of my best creative ideas, frenzied years of hard work, and laughing in the face of everyone who told me I couldn't do it. But after thirteen years, the state of the business was dire. With nowhere to turn and nothing else to try, I listened to my gut and— miraculously, unbelievably, inexplicably—found a way through the chaos to not only save my baby but to scale to new heights.

There have been times when circumstances totally outside of my control have challenged my grip on my sanity—like the pandemic that began in 2020. The isolation, the collective suffering, the polarization of our country, the closure of schools, and the devastation of

New York City . . . the stress and worry became overwhelming. Then I lost my beloved grandmother and struggled to grieve her passing. And *then* there was the fact that I was on camera half the time filming *The Real Housewives of New York*—it was a lot to contend with, and let's be real: maintaining your sobriety while working with Ramona Singer is quite a task even under normal circumstances.

Like so many others, my mental health suffered, and I felt some of my familiar patterns and dangerous behaviors creep into my consciousness. I was suffering from panic attacks and pretending that I wasn't depressed. I felt the ground swell with chaotic energy, and it took everything I had to push through using the tools and wisdom I've gained since the last time I almost lost control. I'm not sure if I'm even capturing how deep the struggle was. If you've dealt with mental health challenges or addiction, you know those moments are beyond intense, and it feels like they'll last forever. You've got to hold on to your sanity like it's a billionaire with a nine-inch dick—to advocate for yourself, do what needs to be done, and never let go.

Some of the best advice I ever got came from the godfather of reality television, Andy Cohen. The day that *RHONY* season twelve was slated to air, my television debut, Andy called me. I was nervous to hear from him directly, but as it turned out, he was reaching out to congratulate me and to hype me up for the premiere—and also to warn me. He said this was the opportunity of a lifetime, but how I handled it was up to me. "Be wise," he said. He told me he's seen fame ruin people's lives, and advised me to stay focused on the things that really matter in my life. It was excellent advice from a guy who has been around the block, or who has actually built the block.

Turns out Andy was right. Fame can be a tricky bitch. I'm happy to say that for the most part, I've done just as he suggested. During the craziest, wildest times when my life felt out of control, I was flailing and panicked as I searched for peace. But I didn't have to run from the discomfort. I would soon learn that tuning in to my instincts and trusting myself over the noise of the crowd would lead me exactly where I needed to go. I learned to trust that the order will appear within the seemingly endless chaos.

Some people thrive under intense conditions; they dial into their inner stillness and their productivity soars. Then there are people like me who create external chaos to distract themselves from the constant inner turmoil. I created chaos to distract myself from the discomfort of facing my fears, pain, disappointments, and anxiety. But when I finally got comfortable enough to live in my own head, I didn't need to create that distraction around me. Maybe when you stop trying to control the world, you can use that energy to thrive in it.

I finally know who I am—or, at least, I'm getting there. I have a good relationship with myself, which is something I never thought I'd be able to say. I've stripped away all of the recklessness that defined my twenties, the self-doubt and anger that pushed me to drink myself away. I recognize that not everyone fits into a neat little box with a neat little label. I have been undefinable for most of my life. I've been the bad girl at a fancy private school; I've been the good girl at a drug-filled Brooklyn rave; I've been a slut and a prude; a liar and a role model; a Catholic and a Jew; a mother and a daughter; a businesswoman and a Housewife. You might think that those identities contradict one another, but they don't. At the end of the day, they've been the same thing all along: me.

CHAPTER 1
THE BUTTERFLY EFFECT

I have come to learn—for better and, sometimes, for worse—that we will never see the thing coming that can change our lives forever. There are watershed moments like giving birth and losing a loved one, breaking up and falling in love, of course, but when it comes to the small moments that lead to a new path, most of the time, they'll surprise you. A missed train, a deal that falls through, a chance encounter, or a split-second decision can impact your whole life. This is the essence of the butterfly effect, one of my favorite parts of chaos theory. The butterfly effect is simply the idea that in nature, tiny changes can lead to completely unexpected and unpredictable results—just like key moments in our own lives can lead us on paths we never imagined.

Seemingly small actions and decisions can create widespread effects.

We can never predict the decisions, innovations, and influences that will change the course of our lives. For me, getting kicked out of school at fourteen years old set me on a different path than I ever imagined for myself. It was my *Sliding Doors* moment as the trajectory of my life changed tracks in an instant. This isn't about what-ifs and living in the past; it's about realizing that, like the flap of a butterfly's wings in one part of the world altering weather patterns in another, seemingly innocuous decisions can impact our lives, and the world around us, in ways we may not see coming. This butterfly moment happened for me in 1996, in the headmistress's office at Convent of the Sacred Heart on the Upper East Side of Manhattan, and I'm still reeling from its effects twenty-five years later.

Tasting the Good Life

I was born and raised in New York City's Chelsea neighborhood, and I was a true New Yorker from the start. I loved the frenetic energy of the city, the endless opportunities and action, and the amalgamation of people. I observed it all from my apartment building on Twenty-

Fourth Street and Eighth Avenue and the hallowed halls of my private school, Sacred Heart, where I was enrolled from third to eighth grade. It's one of the top schools in Manhattan, an all-girls breeding ground for socialites— including my classmates Nikki Hilton and, perhaps less expectedly, Lady Gaga.

I existed as a shape-shifter, fitting in among New York's elite at school and with my neighborhood friends downtown. In my head, the chasm between my classmates and me was vast. I was constantly aware of their money and social status, of their Connecticut country houses and ski chalets, of their closets full of designer clothes and bags. My friends invited me to their lavish vacations, second homes in the Hamptons, after-school shopping trips at Henri Bendel's, and five-star dinners. It was a very different world than what I was used to. My parents were educated and hardworking, but never had *that* kind of money. At some of the most exclusive restaurants in the city, sitting alongside my friend's families, it was trial by fire, and sometimes that meant spilling a glass of orange juice all over a friend's parents, who were the duke and duchess of someplace far away and fancy.

While these divergent experiences have enabled me to walk among many circles as an adult—from basement raves to venture capital boardrooms to Upper East Side haunts—I've felt chronically different, like I've always been adapting in some way. As I got older, and especially as I became sober, it seemed like every alcoholic I met had experience with this feeling of "otherness." There's something about seeing or reacting to the world a little differently from other people that addicts have in common.

To be fair, my classmates at Sacred Heart were perfectly nice; they never said anything to me about me not having what they had. Looking back, I wonder how much of my discomfort was just in my head. I realize now that most middle-school girls feel out of place, after all, unsure in their own skin. It's one of the great joys of adolescence. So maybe it wasn't that I was so different. Maybe we all felt misunderstood on some level.

Even if I didn't know which knife and fork to use with each course, fashion was always my way in. I would get my mom to buy me *Vogue* along with *Seventeen* at the local D'Agostino's when I was twelve, and I'd spend hours devouring the avant-garde looks. While there was a lot I couldn't relate to in *Vogue*, it was my first education on the power and excitement of the fashion industry. By ninth grade, I was wallpapering my bedroom with Versace ads (the Versace ads of the mid-'90s stood out among the crowd in an amazing era of fashion advertising). I was also obsessed with the supermodels of the day, including, of course, the icon Kate Moss.

When you become aware of what you don't have, of the ways in which others are seemingly better off, it can either motivate you or drag you down into feeling less than. I saw the power moms in head-to-toe Chanel, rolling conference calls and making deals while picking up their kids. I saw the lifestyles of my friends—the access to both material wealth and experiential wealth, as well as the endless opportunities. I got a taste of a more glamorous world, and I wanted it one day. Even though the road was paved with junkies, rehabs, and rock bottoms, I eventually clawed my way into it—well, a chic, downtown version of it anyway.

It also gave me a little chip on my shoulder. As a teen, I felt as if I had to rebel against that designer-label, cookie-cutter display of wealth. I wanted a Prada bag like every other teenage girl, but there was no way my parents were going to buy me one even if they could have afforded it (and they couldn't). So I had to make my own way. I bought an orange vinyl tote bag and, using a black Sharpie, I wrote "Prada Sucks" in big bold letters. It was my own experimentation with streetwear before I really know what it was, and it got a lot of attention in school. I think it was a way for me to reject that lifestyle before it rejected me.

I made rejecting it cool, too. One girl lied about where her shoes were from because she was embarrassed to tell me that they were new Miu Miu. I somehow flipped the script from being embarrassed about not having designer goods to making other girls feel embarrassed to show off theirs. I realized in that moment that I possessed the power to manipulate situations in my favor, even if the odds seemed overwhelmingly against me. To gain control even when common sense should dictate otherwise. It's something that has served me well over the years, though in middle school I felt a little guilty for it. I mean, not too guilty. Let's be real: she did have the season's hottest Miu Miu shoes.

The movie *Kids* came out when I was in eighth grade, and, despite its cautionary tale, it set the tone for our social lives going forward. My friends and I dressed in the same skater street style as our new icon, Chloë Sevigny (or maybe she dressed like us!), as we snuck out of our apartments and walked the streets of New York at night, smoking blunts and drinking beer. Whether it was with my school friends or neighborhood friends, it was all the same. Teenagers across the city were quietly escaping their apartments at night, meeting up with friends, and getting into some shit.

We wore uniforms at school, a darker plaid skirt in the fall and winter and a light blue skirt in the spring, paired with a white blouse or polo shirt. As teen girls do, we found ways to bend the rules and express ourselves.

We would roll up our skirts to show a little more leg, tie our white blouses above our navels when the nuns weren't looking. I used Manic Panic to paint bright green streaks in my hair and pierced my belly button. My friends and I would go to Barneys and buy our favorite eyeliners and lip glosses from Make Up For Ever, and they would come downtown with me and shop at my favorite indie stores. Looking back, we were pretty damn sophisticated for a group of thirteen- and fourteen-year-old girls, but of course at the time I felt anything but. In my eighth-grade yearbook you'll find scribbled notes about Gucci bags and trips to Bergdorf's. Not typical for middle schoolers—unless you're in Manhattan.

While my life seemed to be moving along on this path of being the adorable rebel at Sacred Heart, the funny dinner guest at my friend's homes, and the unexpected downtown party girl, I was about to receive a rude awakening.

A Bad Influence

In the fall of eighth grade, my mom received a call from the headmistress saying that she wanted to meet with us both the next day—never a good sign. I thought about everything I had done recently, racking my brain for transgressions, but nothing overt came to mind. There had been an incident with a Bunsen burner earlier that month . . . but surely that couldn't be it.

I swear I can remember every detail from that day. When I arrived at the headmistress's office, my mom was already there. We pushed open the door and entered the office together. The headmistress directed us to sit in a pair of matching antique armchairs positioned directly across from her desk. I fidgeted in my seat and looked around at the hundreds of books lining her shelves.

The headmistress cleared her throat and told us matter-of-factly that I was expelled from Sacred Heart. She said I was a bad influence on my classmates and the school could no longer tolerate my behavior. My mom was quiet. She held her gaze straight ahead as she absorbed the information. The headmistress asked me not to come back after Christmas break, and after some negotiation, my mom convinced her to let me finish the school year. The headmistress must have known how tough it is to change schools midyear, and she agreed to let me stay until June.

We left the office in stunned silence. My face burned with indignation. *I didn't do anything differently than the other girls were doing! Why was she kicking* me *out?* I wanted to scream, but I knew better than to make things worse. My mom looked at me with such disappointment, and it killed me. I had long felt like the faculty of my school treated me differently, and now I was proven right. I was certain their lack of patience with me stemmed from the fact that I wasn't the kind of student they liked to see there. We got partial financial aid. We definitely weren't donating any money. We didn't have a famous last name. There were other girls who did have those last names, and whose families did donate, and I think they had license to act out because they were protected by their money and status. They were above reproach, and they were never disciplined.

If I was hoping for sympathy, I never found it. My parents were pissed, and their disappointment in me was crushing. They didn't see the injustice in the situation— all they saw was an ungrateful daughter who blew her shot at graduating from a good school they'd sacrificed to send her to. They didn't believe that I was being held to a different standard than the other girls. Their lack of faith in me probably hurt more than the fact of being expelled.

For a while, I felt like shit about myself, like I was a piece of trash being thrown away. My thoughts played on a loop, over and over again: *I'm not good enough. What's wrong with me?* For the first time in my life, I felt the full brunt of being rejected for who I am. To this day I can still see the headmistress's look of total disgust as she stared me down from the other side of her desk. I've played that scene over and over in my head more times than I can tell you.

I was also angry. *So* angry. It would take me a while to realize that my best revenge was to become someone who mattered so that no one could treat me like garbage again. They say moments like these are "character building," and truly, I think my expulsion from school shaped me in a fundamental way. Anyone who knows me today knows I'm quick to stand up for myself—floating like a butterfly—but willing to sting like a bitch. I never again want to feel like that young girl felt.

My final semester of school was tense. I was licking my wounds and wondering where I fit it. The teachers all knew I'd been expelled, and they seemed to treat me even more harshly. Why would they invest any more time and effort in my learning when I'd be gone in a few months? It did so much damage to my self-esteem.

As I got down on myself for screwing up my opportunity at Sacred Heart, for disappointing my parents, and for being the kind of kid who could be so easily discarded, I also became more critical of my appearance. As a preteen and teen, I always felt ugly. I could easily write a laundry list of complaints about my physical appearance: I had acne, muscular legs, a gap in my teeth, and so on. It seemed easier to focus on my physical woes instead of the whirlwind of emotions and doubts in my head. Now I look back at pictures from eighth grade and I see a cute, awkward girl who was struggling to fit in. It's always that way, isn't it? In the moment, you have a million complaints about the way you look; years later, you can't believe you wasted so much energy being so mean to yourself. Of course, that's something I'm working on. I'm still my harshest critic. The difference is that now I have a much healthier, more realistic self-image, even if it's not perfect. I've come to learn that self-criticism and lack of confidence are rarely only about your physical appearance, and being self-conscious is human. But that perspective is hard won, and not easily accessed when you're a teenage girl. (Well, unless you're Ivanka Trump, whom I remember seeing at a friend's thirteenth birthday party. She looked every bit the part: rich and pretty, confident and comfortable in her skin, like she had access to everything she might want. Say what you want about her now, but at age thirteen, the girl was stunning. Also, for the record, she offered me a ride home from the party in her limo, but when I told her where I lived, she said, "Never mind.")

A Change Will Do
Us Good

The ramifications of my expulsion were finally realized in earnest when the school year ended and my parents told me we were leaving the city. They sat me, my brother, and my sister in the living room and told us they had bought a house in Newtown, Connecticut, an hour and a half outside the city. I was shocked. The news came as a physical blow, as if I'd been sucker punched. I didn't know much, but I knew I belonged in New York City.

My siblings and I had very little warning before our lives were uprooted—we moved just a couple months later. Our parents didn't show us the new house or town before we left. They simply told us it was happening and gave us some boxes to pack our shit. I asked over and over why we were moving, and my parents said it was because I got thrown out of Sacred Heart and they had nowhere else to send me, which was total bullshit. I could have gone to the local public school in Chelsea. But my mom had a job opportunity in a neighboring Connecticut town, and my parents wanted to get out of the city. I get it. New York City is incredibly expensive, and private school for three kids was an impossibility. In hindsight, I know they were making what felt like the best choice not only for me but for my brother and sister—for all of us as a family. But wasn't there something in between the Big Apple and Nowheresville, Connecticut?

I seemed like my life was over, and there was absolutely nothing I could do about it. I felt helpless and alone, unable to confide in anyone. My parents and I became completely disconnected, and I stopped caring if I disappointed them or not. So instead of being honest and vulnerable, I started acting out more. That's when things began to take a turn for me. I think a healthy fear of disappointing your parents helps you stay out of trouble as a kid. Not me. I became so resentful that I ended up doing the opposite—I was seeking out ways to disappoint them, to show them what bad behavior really looked like.

Newtown, Connecticut, was rural. *Really* rural. Our house was an old converted barn, which I now think is beautiful. But at the time, I was shocked by the stark difference to our small but modern tenth-floor apartment with views of the Empire State Building. I missed the faint sound of traffic lulling me to sleep at night. I missed the independence of walking out my front door and having the whole city at my fingertips. I had lived in one of the liveliest neighborhoods in the city, maybe even the world, with an abundance of restaurants and bars, incredible shopping, and sidewalks bustling with people from all walks of life. In Connecticut, all I had was a general store, a $2 movie theater, and a big flag-pole in the center of the road. It was a suburban night-mare.

I had such independence in New York. I could walk or take the subway everywhere I wanted to go, and that meant that I never had to rely on anyone, especially my parents. But in the suburbs, of course, it wasn't that easy. I didn't yet have a driver's license, so I made friends with older kids with cars, or I'd beg my parents to drive me to the mall. Getting anywhere felt like a chore.

I'm sure for some people, suburban Connecticut is a dream come true. But I didn't care about having a back-yard or exploring the great parks and trails in our area. I wanted culture, the excitement of nightlife and restau-rants, and options to go shopping. What I got instead was the Danbury Fair Mall, which had one skate store that I frequented. Nothing about the fluorescent lights and smell of food court pizza felt like a good trade from my favorite downtown boutiques. Luckily I had enough clothes to last me awhile.

Sometimes I wonder if the headmistress of my school ever realized the effect she had on my life. Her decision changed the circumstances of an entire family, and it set me on a course that would come to define who I am. I'm not blaming her or suggesting that anything I went through in the ensuing decade(s) was her fault, or the fault of any one person or situation. We are all the sum of our actions, and mine got me to a place where I lost my sense of belonging, my sense of safety, my sense of identity. I felt abandoned and vengeful. And there are few things more chaotic than an angry teenager with nothing to lose.

CHAPTER 2
HURRICANE
LEAH

A storm was brewing inside as I struggled to find my footing in our new town. The impact of my being expelled and our leaving New York City resulted in a period of time spent in the eye of the storm . . . of the century. The moodiness, unpredictability, and impulsive behavior of teenagers often serve as inspiration in pop culture. It makes for great songs, compelling movies, and the kind of angsty books that stay with you for a lifetime. The undeveloped prefrontal cortex and raging hormones are commonly held responsible for teens' erratic behavior, emotional outbursts, and poor decision-making. What happens if you add in the soul-shattering experience of rejection, the frustration of feeling misunderstood and isolated, and a serious amount of anger? Well, the results are pretty fucking volatile.

I started my new high school in Newtown, Connecticut, with a sense of doomsday determination to hate it as much as possible. I wanted to spite my parents for ruining my life—my siblings were adjusting well to the move, but I wouldn't let my mom and dad off so easily. I would guess looking back that I also, on some level, wanted to punish myself for getting expelled in the first place, though as a pissed-off thirteen-year-old that wasn't exactly a conscious thought.

At the time, I'd already experimented with alcohol. I started earlier that year, sneaking out and sipping beers with my friends as we walked around the muggy New York City streets in the summer. We hid our beers in unmarked brown paper bags and smoked cigarettes, feeling rebellious and wild and free. I blacked out and threw up all over myself the first time I got drunk. I saw no issue with it. In my twisted head, it was fun. It didn't become a problem until I got a little older. I wanted to do anything that would get me out of my own head for a while, and so I drank more and more as I ran further and further from myself.

Finding the Beat

When I started high school, I was quick to make friends, at least superficially. One of the first friends I made was a kindred spirit in the form of a girl named Alex, who lived just down the street from me. Alex was tall and lanky, with a mischievous smile and big brown eyes. She wasn't overly chatty, but I could tell she was genuine. Plus, she was from Westchester—the county in New York State just north of the city—so I felt like I had more in common with her than my classmates. She had NYC taste, and I was pulled toward her like a magnet. We spent our days smoking joints, looking through *Vogue*, worshipping Kate Moss, and listening to Deee-Lite. We also got into a lot of trouble together—smoking in the bathroom, getting high, and drinking by the train tracks. There were many detentions and suspensions. I was bored with all of the kids in my town, who I thought were sheltered and naive, and I was uncomfortable in my own skin. Alex became my outlet and my saving grace.

Even though I had a friend, I struggled to adjust to my new life. I was drinking a lot, and I was doing any drug anyone would give me, including huffing Glade air fresheners. We would put a hand towel over a can of Glade, spray it, and inhale. It would, of course, smell like whatever citrus or peony bullshit our moms bought, but we could get high from it. It was disgusting, and it's honestly embarrassing to admit it now. But at the time, I just wanted to lose myself in the not-feeling, not-caring bliss of being high.

By this point, I was smoking weed every day. Alex and I were also doing acid whenever we could get our hands on it—which was more often than you might think for two teenage girls living in the New England sticks. When I was fourteen, I tried crystal meth, and I felt like a goddamn superwoman. I felt like I was tapped into my higher consciousness instead of flailing around a sweaty dance floor with a bunch of teenagers. I thought I was hiding all of this partying from my parents, but looking back, I can only imagine the kinds of bizarre things I was saying and doing.

In the middle of freshman year, Alex and I went to our first official rave at the now-closed Roseland Ballroom. We went with another girl, Morgan, whom Alex knew from an outpatient drug treatment program. (I wonder if this was the peer group my parents had in mind when they moved us to a sweet Connecticut town.) That night, I took acid and speed together, and I loved it. I felt electrified, eyes wide open, heart pounding, carefree. It was a big jump from beer, weed, and cigarettes, but I was all in. I could feel every single beat of the music shoot into my pores and enter my bloodstream, connecting everyone on the dance floor as if we were all one single organism. I forgot who I was there. Or maybe I became who I was there. It doesn't matter. I fell in love with the bass, the freedom, the drugs, the giant Polo Sport rugbies, dancing till nine in the morning. The only time I didn't feel like an alien was in a dark club with the music pounding.

I *loved* Roseland, especially the bathrooms there. Any raver or club kid knows that the real party was always in the bathrooms. The Roseland bathrooms were my favorite because of the soft, flattering lighting and the sheer size of the things. They were huge, and the perfect place for us to recharge, meet new friends, do our drugs, and reapply our Mac Lipglass and Versace Red Jeans perfume. There was even a room off to the side with couches, which always came in handy when sniffing too much K. It's where we would congregate to talk and actually hear one another.

I was uncontrollable, spiraling in misery and isolation, doing anything I could to escape my pain. Ironically, the one thing that felt like my salvation—partying all night at raves, absorbing love and community from a crowded dance floor—also became my downfall.

Appetite for Destruction

My freshman year of high school ended, giving way to the wide-open stretch of summer with little structure. I took advantage of it—partying for days at a time with my friends and going into the city more frequently. Toward the end of the summer, I went to another rave at Roseland Ballroom, but this time I stayed in the city partying for four days straight. I don't even know where I was most of that time.

After my days-long bender, I finally went home. My parents were furious; no surprise there. But I was in for a surprise soon enough. A couple of weeks later, after the school year was underway, instead of heading to school in the morning, my parents rolled out a suitcase they'd secretly packed and announced that they were driving me to rehab. I stayed calm (we can thank my massive hangover for that) and told them that I would look at the rehab for a day or so, but I wouldn't be staying, and they seemed to agree. I sat in the back seat reading *Valley of the Dolls* the whole four-hour drive to Caron Foundation in Wernersville, Pennsylvania.

When we arrived and took a tour of the facilities, my parents promised they would come back the next day to get me. I asked my dad for a pack of Newports because I ran out, and he bought me a carton instead. It was only after they drove off that I realized I had a month's worth of cigarettes, and that I would be there to smoke every one of them.

Still, I told the kids on the unit that I would be staying for only a couple of days. I was in for a rude awakening when they informed me that it would be at least a week before I could even make a phone call to my parents. I didn't talk to anyone for that first week. I refused to participate in groups, I barely ate, I cried for the first time in a year. I had been too angry about the expulsion and the move to really grieve; I didn't feel like I could let my guard down. But in that rehab facility—oh, my G-d, did I cry. I didn't want to look like a pussy in front of a bunch of strangers, but I couldn't help it. The jig was up. I was not some hard-ass, I was a kid in a lot of pain, stuck in addiction.

Halfway through my stay at Caron, my parents came to a family weekend for two days of group therapy and activities. The whole experience was very intense. For my parents, seeing the other kids there who were really struggling was eye-opening. In our big group session, each of us had a turn with our family in the center of the circle to discuss our issues with the help and support of the others. The energy was so heavy as everyone unpacked these difficult personal histories. My mom was the one to sit in a metal folding chair in the middle of the circle with me. My dad struggled that weekend, and he spent a lot of time back at the hotel. I think the reality of seeing me in rehab was very difficult for him to face, and I had a lot more compassion for him after seeing how deeply affected he was by the whole scene.

As my mom sat across from me, she shared her experiences dealing with my addiction in front of a group of near strangers. To hear her say aloud how I'd hurt my family, how I'd disappointed her, and how much pain I'd caused her was overwhelming. I told her I didn't know why I did what I did. I didn't have much insight to offer her in the moment. I was fighting a disease that turns you into a selfish asshole, which makes it damn hard to get sympathy or understanding from people.

At fifteen years old, it was the most emotionally intense experience of my life, but the most important takeaway for me was discovering that there were some depression issues in my family—something no one had ever told me. I learned that much of addiction is a disease and a cycle that can transfer down from generation to generation, often for reasons unknown. Even if I didn't totally understand what addiction was or how it functions, I knew I had it.

After twenty-eight days of treatment, my parents picked me up, brought me home, and I went back to school. Now, I was not only the weirdo girl from New York City; I was also the crackhead who'd spent the first month of school in a rehab. I was stared at in my classes, and I heard kids talking about me under their breath in the hallways.

As if that wasn't bad enough, while I was at Caron,

my parents signed me over to the state of Connecticut as part of their PINS (person in need of supervision) program. So when I returned home, I had a probation officer to report to for regular drug testing. If I failed a test, I would be sent to a juvenile detention center. Talk about a tough-love approach. I felt another stab of betrayal as my parents continued to strip me of autonomy and freedom at a time when that's what I wanted most. This kind of supervision did keep me clean for about eight months, until I found a way around the system. When I did start using again, I got clean urine from kids in town. I would take the filled cup and put it in my sock under my wide-leg jeans. When I went to my probation meeting for a drug test, I'd dump the clean urine into the cup they gave me. I kept this up for a few months until I turned sixteen and aged out of the program.

I had so many hard-partying nights as a teenager, often putting myself in wild and dangerous situations that stemmed from following the party and the drugs wherever they would take me. I don't know why I was so self-destructive. Maybe I was born an addict. Maybe I was looking for relief from my pain. Maybe I was creating outward chaos to drown out the inner chaos. Whatever the reason, sometimes I think that if I hadn't found raves and drugs to dull my pain I would've killed myself. In a way, they were a lifesaver.

Until they weren't.

One night, I went into the city to go to one of my favorite clubs, Carbon. Usually when I went out I would lie to my parents and say I was sleeping over at the home of whatever nice girl from my town they would be okay with. Then I'd call a cab to take me to the bus station or to the train station and go into the city, where I'd meet up with childhood friends and hit the clubs. But on this night, I was flying solo. Even when I couldn't get someone to come with me, I was never deterred from finding a party. Everyone knew everyone on the club-kid circuit, and I was sure I'd run into friends when I got there.

That night, I called my parents from a pay phone in the city and said, "I'm not coming home. I'm not going to be in school tomorrow. You're not going to see me. I'm just gone. Don't even look for me." Could you imagine what my mother must have thought when she got that call? I don't know what came over me. But when I got into the city, I just couldn't imagine going back. I didn't even pack a bag. I had the clothes on my back and a couple of bucks in my pocket to get into the club. That was it.

I showed up at Carbon on the early side—around midnight—because I had nowhere else to go. I set out to make some friends and find some familiar faces, as any good addict does. That particular night I caught up with some people who introduced me to Special K and crystal meth combined. You mix the two powders into one line and sniff it. What a combo! It was probably the best high I've ever had.

Nothing compares to your first high on a new drug. See, there are different kinds of speed. When I did speed for the first time at a rave, it was okay only because it was overpowered by the acid I'd already taken. But the first time that I did crystal meth was truly insane. I felt like I had just never been happier in my entire life. It was as though I was experiencing a head-to-toe full-body orgasm. I thought my face might explode from smiling. It felt like rainbows were flying through my bloodstream. It never felt like that again. There's never another first time.

I literally chased that feeling for years. That's how a lot of addicts are born. You try it once and feel this unbelievable way. I didn't want to go back to reality ever again. I wanted to stay in that place—high, on the dance floor, for hours. *Happy.*

After that night at Carbon, true to my word, I didn't go home for a week. I met this sweet girl named Angel at six A.M., and she asked where I was going next. I told her I didn't have anywhere to go, and she invited me to stay with her. We took a train to her place in the Bronx.

It started snowing, and I was not dressed for the weather. I was freezing as I followed her from the subway to her apartment, which she shared with her grandmother. The next day, she gave me some subway tokens, twenty dollars in cash, and even a North Face jacket. Angel was, in fact, an angel.

After my night in the Bronx, I needed somewhere to stay, so I called a friend who put me in touch with her older sister, who then put me in touch with her ex-boyfriend, whose name was Revolution. He lived in Brooklyn, and I hid out in his apartment for the rest of the week. He and his roommate were there, and mostly they were amused by my antics, but they also looked out for me like I was their actual little sister. I called my parents occasionally to tell them I was okay and found out the police were looking for me. I refused to tell them where I was, despite their tears and anguish. I finally came home after about a week when I realized my new living quarters weren't going to be sustainable.

My life was so bleak that I was willing to sleep on the couch of a random guy named Revolution. That's saying something. Thank G-d he ended up being so cool. I wouldn't let myself slow down long enough to take stock of the decisions I was making. I was focused only on searching for the next party, the next drug, and the next distraction. When the music was loud, or when the high was taking over, I couldn't hear my own thoughts, which was just how I liked it.

Unfortunately for me, I could not stop fucking up my life. I was expelled for the rest of sophomore year from Newtown High School after getting into a fight with another girl. She had called my older boyfriend a child molester, and I threw her up against a locker. That was it for me. Instead of going to school, I was tutored a couple hours a day as part of a program that the town provided for "kids like me." I spent my afternoons watching *Jerry Springer* and *Days of Our Lives* with my grandma Cele, who was living with us. It was a sad existence. After a while, I saw no point in staying sober anymore.

To this day, I'm not clear on the purpose of expelling students. It seems like schools are taking the most troubled, vulnerable kids and doing the exact opposite of what they need—singling them out and sending them away, instead of embracing them and supporting their pain. I was a week out of rehab at fifteen years old, and I was struggling as I dealt with the emotional fallout of going back to school. The administration could have been more understanding to a girl who was clearly struggling. I guess it's a tough-love approach, but tough love never worked for me.

Only Green Lights

I returned to school for my junior year, and I was able to just barely hold it together—more or less—for the rest of high school and graduated by the skin of my teeth. I basically begged my guidance counselor and principal to let me graduate. I didn't have enough attendance days, but I had a meeting with them, and I leveled with them: "Look, I do not belong here. I cannot stay here for another day in this school or in this town. Let me get my high school diploma and get out of here." And they did. They were actually reasonable, stand-up guys to look at my life as a whole and acknowledge that I knew what I needed.

Most people react to addiction with a lot more judgment than that. Even now, after it was a story line on my first season of *RHONY*, I faced judgment from other Housewives and plenty from viewers, too. The battle with this disease is lifelong, and one of its challenges is the stigma and misconceptions that come along with it.

Addicts don't have a red light in their brain, only a green light. Once I tried drugs and alcohol, that green light clicked on for me. I knew that my brain wasn't able to handle it the same way other people could. My friends, who had partied with me, were able to go to college and live their lives normally. Watching them find that balance between their academic lives and their partying made me realize that I was an addict.

If I felt a deep loss of self-worth when I got expelled from Sacred Heart, it was matched by my feelings as I watched the optimism and promise on display as the freshly graduated seniors prepared for college while I stood on the sidelines. People compared notes on where they were applying and who heard from what school. Still, I knew that college wasn't for me. I was eager to get back to the city where I felt most myself, and that vision didn't include sitting in a lecture hall. And, just in case I wasn't sure if I belonged at college or not, my parents confirmed that they weren't going to waste their money on tuition.

It was the right decision, but that didn't mean it wasn't absolutely depressing. I felt like I was on a terrible path, all alone. Everyone I knew packed up and headed off to their new adventures while I stayed at my parents' house in small-town Connecticut and hung out with my rave friends, going to clubs in the city, drinking myself into oblivion, and smoking PCP.

My peers seemed to have their whole lives ahead of them; I was stuck in the same loop of going to a rave or a party, doing everything I could get my hands on to numb myself, and recovering under the heavy weight of morning-after remorse.

The Tough-Love Approach

A few months after graduating and partying nonstop, I realized I couldn't keep going on with my life the way it was. I couldn't sustain that level of drinking and drug use. I felt dead inside. So, I did what I would have thought unthinkable a few years before: I asked my parents to help me go back to rehab. At just eighteen years old, it would be my third stint in rehab. That's right; there was a quick trip to a detox facility in Putnam County during my junior year of high school, but that rehab proved much less effective for me. There was practically no supervision at the time, and I spent most of my twenty-eight days sharing meds, blasting music, and dancing all night with the other fun-loving addicts.

Five years after my first sip of booze and my entire existence had become ruled by substances. I wasn't thrilled to be back at Caron, but I knew the faces, and I felt a certain level of comfort there. I'm not sure that familiarity is a real selling point at rehab, but it felt like a place I could start to get back on track. I knew that I could get support at Caron, and, for the first time that I can remember, I wanted to be helped. My parents did not return to Caron for another family weekend; they'd been through it once, and they felt that was enough. After another ninety days filled with group therapy sessions and activities like dodgeball, movie night, and even indoor rock climbing, I was feeling much stronger and ready to go home.

The problem was, after rehab, my parents didn't want me to come home. After so many years of coping with the complete insanity brought on by my drug use and drinking, my mom, Bunny, finally said enough is enough. She needed to protect the family. I was devastated to think that my family needed protection from me. Even now that I'm a mom, and I recognize why she did what she did, it still devastates me. Being thrown out of my house is one of the most intense feelings of rejection I'd ever experienced. I tried to remind myself that my addiction was the danger, not me, but I resented my mother a lot.

I held on to that hurt and pain for a long time, until I went to therapy and did some work on myself. I finally realized that this decision was the biggest gift my mother ever gave me. She set a firm boundary that forced me to take responsibility for my life. I could have continued skating by, drinking when I was in pain, and taking shelter in my small Connecticut bedroom when the world (or the hangover) became too much. Until that moment, when I had to figure it out for myself.

After I got over the initial shock, I asked my mom, "Where am I supposed to go?" She'd found a place for me at a therapeutic community run by nuns in upstate New York called New Hope. I agreed to go only because I had nowhere else to turn. When I finished rehab, my parents picked me up in their minivan and drove me to New Hope while I slept. They dropped me off and, as I watched them drive away, I stood proudly and gave them the middle finger.

New Hope was a run-down treatment center that looked like an abandoned compound for a cult. It's in the middle of nowhere, along the New York–Pennsylvania border. Everyone had been court-mandated to be there, except for me—it's safe to say that I didn't feel like I fit in. My first day was miserable. I mean soul-shatteringly miserable. At my first seminar, everyone was silently working on their treatment plans or school assignments. I hated the silence, which seemed forced and restricting. I felt it churning in my stomach and stinging my hands. Truthfully, I felt the same way that I did when we first moved to that quiet Connecticut suburb from busy, loud New York City: it made me want to get fucked up.

When you arrive at New Hope, the nuns take almost everything away from you, down to your underwear, and you have to earn it back. One of the nuns was named Sister Marie, and another was named Sister Cecilia, which are my grandmothers' names. In an effort to be optimistic, I kept telling myself that it was a sign from G-d that I needed to stay there, that I was where I was meant to be, but it was pretty hard to keep the faith. I was assigned the top bunk of a dismal room with a woman whose snores would shake the whole bed. I thought the bed frame was going collapse on top of her.

All of the shock, the despair, the bargaining, the rationalizing was a struggle that took place over the first twenty-four hours. On my second night, I tried to escape. I crawled out the bathroom window to find one of the nuns staring at me. I started laughing and ran around the building, walking back in through the front door. They must give you one free pass for attempted escape, because there were no repercussions.

It took three days to break me. On my third day, I announced I was leaving. I told my therapist, "I'm eighteen years old, and you are holding me hostage. You need to give me my stuff, or I'm leaving without it." She called my parents and told them she had to release me; legally, she couldn't make me stay. I got my stuff and caught a Greyhound bus back to the city, where I knew I belonged.

You could say I've always done things my own way. This stubbornness has been one of my greatest assets, and for a while, it was my biggest vulnerability. It's what made me call my mom and tell her I wasn't coming home for a week; it's what made me want to show the world what a bad kid I could be. But it's also how I eventually dug myself out of that hole to build my life on my own terms. There was no one who could live my life for me, and no one—not my parents or the nuns of upstate New York—could decide what was best for me. I was willing to live with the consequences as long as I could call my own shots.

Back in the New York Groove

When I got back to New York, I stayed with my good friend Abby and her father, Ned, at their apartment on 103rd Street and West End Avenue. It was my second home for most of my childhood, and I felt comfortable there. But after a few weeks of my sleeping till noon, Ned woke me up one day with a glass of fresh-squeezed orange juice and politely told me to get my shit together.

It was just the kick in the ass I needed. I found a halfway house on Seventeenth Street between Third Avenue and Lexington run by Hazelden, a really good rehab program. *And* they accepted my insurance. (Thank you, Dad!) I moved in and lived there for the summer. One year after high school graduation, I was nineteen, trying to stay sober for the second time (or was it the third?), and living in a halfway house. I had wanted to move back to New York—but not like this.

The Hazelden halfway house was very nice for what it was. It was located in a big, beautiful brownstone in Gramercy Park, an exclusive neighborhood. Amanda Lepore lived at Hotel 17 next door, and we saw her on the block all the time. We had the support and supervision we needed to transition from rehab to real life. We had a curfew, we were drug-tested, and we went to daily group therapy, where the conversation ranged from past traumas and near overdoses to minor transgressions of roommates leaving clothing on the wrong side of the room. We shared bedrooms, four or five to a room. There was no privacy, and the women there were intense. One of my roommates was a sex addict, and she spent her days running around town finding guys to fuck in Starbucks bathrooms. Honestly, I really felt for her. I went on a date one night, and the guy walked me home to the halfway house. It definitely kills the mood.

Residents were required to keep a job, so I got a part-time gig at the Guess store in Soho. It seemed as good a place as any to bide my time, if only by folding overpriced T-shirts and ringing up customers. I was happy enough with this little routine—until I came down with walking pneumonia. I needed space to be alone and to recover. Against the advice of the Hazelden staff, I

checked into St. Mark's Hotel in the East Village to re-
cuperate. And once I experienced the peace and quiet of
a room of my own, I knew I had to leave Hazelden. It
was just too overwhelming for me to be around so many
people all the time. So I called my grandmother, who
lived in a rent-controlled studio in the same building I
grew up in. It took some convincing, but eventually, re-
luctantly, she agreed to take me in.

When I moved back to Chelsea, I finally felt like I
was getting my shit together. I decided to try my hand
at what everyone else my age seemed to be doing: going
to school. I signed up for a few credit cards to buy some
classes at the Fashion Institute of Technology (and a
J'Adore Dior sleeveless tee that was the iconic look of the
moment). But my earlier instincts about school had been
right; after just a few days of lecture halls, professors,
and syllabi, I knew it wasn't for me. I didn't want to sit in
a classroom and be talked at. My courses—photography
and advertising—interested me in theory, but I couldn't
get on board with the academic approach to artistic, creative subjects. I remember doing an advertising project
for a faux cologne, where I featured work from the artist
Dash Snow and graffiti artist Earsnot. It was cutting-
edge and timely, but the professor didn't get it. (Though
I would be vindicated years later when every luxury
brand in the world was chasing Dash Snow [RIP].) Suf-

fice to say: I quit school after a few months. It felt point-less to be graded on something as subjective as creativity, but I think it was worth the credit card debt to figure that out for myself. Ultimately, I proved to myself that not going to college was the right choice. But that didn't bring me any closer to knowing what I did want to do.

CHAPTER 3
SPONTANEOUS ORDER

Sometimes opportunities emerge not as the result of careful planning, but because, in life, crazy shit happens. I entered my twenties in a state of utter chaos, and I ended the decade with a successful business and a five-year-old daughter. I came an incredibly long way in those years, and yet, most of that time, I still wasn't exactly sure of what I was doing. I threw myself into starting a business with no experience, into parenting while battling alcoholism, and into finding myself through a haze of booze and prescription meds. I just kept moving forward, staying in motion until I figured it out. I had to try things and fail or reject them in order to figure out what made sense for me.

That meant a lot of false starts, but it also left me open

to new people and ideas, and the ability to jump into a situation with no expectations. Through failed jobs and internships, drunk conversations in the back booth of a bar, or meeting someone's cousin's friend's neighbor at just the right moment, I was able to explore fashion and streetwear, art and music, and learn enough to start knowing what I liked. All of these experiences were my education. Instead of sitting in lecture halls with professors handing out stapled packets of reading assignments, I walked the streets of lower Manhattan with graffiti artists and streetwear innovators. Instead of studying abroad through an exchange program, I traveled with crazy ex-boyfriends and fashion moguls to see parts of the world I'd always dreamed of. It may have been a harder and longer and more circuitous path than some people can stomach, but it was right for me. And it allowed me to create my clothing line, Married to the Mob.

My teenage years were defined by pain and self-harm. I got high to escape, but doing drugs became about more than that. It became my identity. It became my best friend. And despite the early success of MTTM, the pull toward drugs and alcohol became the biggest roadblock to living the kind of life that I wanted to live. Finally, two unexpected aha moments helped me get sober and seek support for my mental pain. One brought me face-to-face with G-d; the other brought me face-to-face with mortality.

The Biggest Decision of My Life

By my early twenties, I'd had friends who had gotten pregnant, but none of them had had a baby. The world I was in didn't have a lot of young women starting families in their twenties like you might see in other areas of the country. New York City in 2004 was home to a career-focused, status-obsessed generation of twenty-somethings.

So at twenty-four, when I found myself peeing on a pregnancy-test stick in the bathroom of the apartment I shared with my boyfriend, Rob, I was hoping for a negative test. This wasn't my first pregnancy scare. Rob and I had been living together for four years by then, and we weren't always as careful as we should have been.

As I waited the two excruciating minutes for the results, I thought about my business and how after a couple of years, we were really gaining some traction. Top boutiques all over the world were requesting line sheets, and my brand was getting a ton of press. Who knew a teenage delinquent whose life had been a blur of drugs, after-hours parties, and halfway houses could make something out of herself? I was proud of the company and the direction my life was going in. I knew the results of this test could change everything.

Two minutes crawled by. I walked back into the bathroom and looked at the stick. *It's a fucking plus sign.* I thought, *Maybe that means not pregnant?* I dug through the garbage to find the box for instructions, and I confirmed that plus does, in fact, mean pregnant.

My heart was pounding, and I immediately felt dizzy. I sat down on the edge of the tub as my mind raced: *What is my mom going to say? I can't keep this baby. I'm just getting started with MTTM. I have options, don't I?* I calmed myself down and I called my sister, Rob, and my mom, in that order. Which meant that the first reaction I heard was my sister telling me, with equal degrees of excitement and concern in her voice, that if I wanted an abortion she would fly home from her Abercrombie shoot to be with me. (Love you, Auntie Sarah!)

When I got Rob on the phone, I blurted out the news and waited for him to react. There was no hesitation from him, just pure positivity and happiness. I'll never forget how confidently he said, "We got this, Leah." I was pretty shocked by Rob's reaction, given that I was basically hyperventilating. But then again, Rob is the most laid-back guy I've ever known.

My mom, meanwhile, had deep concern in her voice as she told me, "You're about to make the biggest decision of your life." I have already shared this with my daughter, and she knows that I was not exactly prepared to have a child (I'm still kind of not!) and, yes, I had fleeting thoughts of terminating. But I very quickly realized that wasn't what I wanted. I decided to keep the baby, and to become a mother. I took the test on a Friday, and on Monday went to my ob-gyn. I had a sonogram, and at six weeks I saw the flickering of my daughter's heartbeat. Any doubts I had evaporated after that.

It was the unexpected choice. But it felt right to me. Rob was confident we could handle it, and I felt like I had the support to do it. I didn't overthink it. Sarah was supportive. My mother was elated. My dad, after making a joke about murdering Rob, was thrilled. My friends were all happy for me when they heard the news.

I embraced the pregnancy and felt a sense of readiness wash over me. It was overwhelming and daunting at times, sure, but it also felt like it was meant to be. I had no problem staying sober. It was a little surprising to me that it wasn't an issue at all, but it just . . . wasn't. As I prepared to have a baby, I was also happily focused on

nurturing my other firstborn—MTTM—which continued to grow. I felt busy and purposeful during my
pregnancy. Of course, I missed out on some late-night
partying and trips with my friends, which was hard
sometimes. But I also felt like I was right where I was
meant to be.

When I got pregnant at twenty-four as an unmarried,
not-sober woman just beginning to get her young adult
life together, conventional wisdom might have said that
it wasn't the time for me to become a mother. But I felt in
my bones that I was ready. I let go of the idea of having a perfect family that checked all of the boxes and
embraced the fact that this was the family I was meant
to have. When you release those expectations, fears, and
the need to do things a certain way, so much possibility
opens itself up to you.

Kier was born exactly on her due date on June 1, 2007,
at St. Vincent's Hospital in the West Village, which is
now an ugly luxury rental building made of fake-looking
brick. I had a natural childbirth, and I labored for a total of twenty-four hours and pushed for three. It's crazy
what women do to bring life into this world! It was the
most intense physical pain I've ever experienced, and if
I ever do it again, I will have no hesitation about getting an epidural. Kier was born at 11:06 A.M. and looked
perfect. She was placed on my chest and stared up at me

while searching for my nipple with her mouth. I was just in awe. It was the closest to G-d I have ever been. I don't think I even said anything. I just stared.

Postpartum Booze

I gave birth on a Friday, and Rob went to work the following Monday. I was breastfeeding around the clock and alone for most of the day until Rob got home from work at around six P.M. Rob's parents offered to pay for a baby nurse, but I scoffed. I refused to hire any help. I insisted on doing it on my own. I had this urgent sense that I needed to be alone with Kier to bond with her, and I thought that if I did it all myself in those first few weeks, I was being a good mother. All the while, I was still running MTTM—no maternity leave for me! When you run your own company, there's no time off— and the truth is, I welcomed the distraction and the opportunity to feel in my element.

Some of that time was beautiful. As I sat in the rocking chair and nursed Kier, I would look at her tiny wrinkled hands or her big, dark eyes and marvel at how small and beautiful and fragile she was—and maybe that life was, too. I was struck by such an overwhelming feeling of love for her; I couldn't believe it existed. The days and nights would swing between these tender moments of awe and devotion and, basically, the desire to climb the walls.

The combination of isolation and exhaustion eventually led to a state of total overwhelm. Of course, experiencing anything other than pure joy to be with my baby made me feel guilty and ashamed, which triggered my desire to drink. But this time I couldn't numb the pain; I had a newborn to take care of. And on top of that, my work was essential to our family's income, so I knew I couldn't take my foot off the gas of building my business. I don't know if it was because I was a young mom, or because running MTTM was so demanding, or because I was still *me* underneath the cloak of motherhood, but I grappled with the responsibility of being a working mom while wanting to live my life and enjoy my freedom. My attention was split, and the inner struggle exhausted me.

Some days, it was all I could do to go through the motions. Eventually, I figured out how to go out and drink from time to time to take the edge off. I would tell Rob that I had a "work dinner" or a networking opportunity, but really I just wanted to get out of the house and have a few cocktails (well, actually, more like ten Belvedere dirty martinis, but you get the point). Rob picked up the slack for me, taking amazing care of Kier as I struggled to find balance.

As the weeks stretched to months, I became more and more distraught. I honestly don't know whether I had postpartum depression, or regular depression, or if the reality of being a mom was finally sinking in. Maybe I'd always felt like this, but I just never knew. I had spent so many years masking my emotions with drugs and booze, the sobriety of my pregnancy and first postpartum months allowed me to actually feel my feelings. I loved Kier so much, but I was a mess. I had intrusive, terrifying thoughts of accidentally dropping her down the stairs of our building that constantly haunted me.

As soon as I stopped breastfeeding, I started going out regularly—drinking vodka sodas, champagne with Chambord, and wine. It may sound perfectly innocuous, but it's all about quantity. You're not supposed to drink twelve glasses of wine at dinner. And then, of course, there was the coke and the pills, too. I was back to "high school Leah," taking whatever people gave me to run from myself. I was always on the edge of going berserk, and drinking gave me the ability to let go. At the time, it felt like I was constantly holding myself back from an all-out bender. Even today, I'm still on that ledge and need to be aware of it so that I don't fall off. It's less of a drop, but it's still there.

My memories of the first couple years of Kier's life are a blur. My drinking created a huge rift between me and Rob, and while he didn't always articulate how angry he was, the resentments were clear. We began to grow further and further apart—while loving our daughter more and more every day. As Kier's second birthday approached, I was increasingly distracted by my need to go out and drink, and the subsequent nagging guilt that I should be home. I refused to admit that I needed professional help, so instead I sought the advice of a psychic . . . who told me that I would be better off not drinking. Maybe I was looking for someone to tell me what I already knew.

My drinking continued to escalate. I would come home at five A.M. blackout drunk something like twice a week. By that time I'd hired a nanny, so I just had to survive the mornings until she arrived. There is nothing darker than waking up to take care of your baby and throwing up from the night before. Rob would film me when I got home from a night out and threaten to use it against me. All we did was fight—sober or otherwise. I was not present for my daughter in the way I always dreamed I would be. The unsettling reality of that is what finally pushed me to start therapy.

Gifts of Desperation

I first saw my therapist, Barbara, in September 2009. My life was a disaster. Actually, my life looked decent from the outside—thriving business, beautiful daughter, the appearance of success and happiness—but behind the facade, things were bleak. I was having panic attacks while drunk. Rob and I had split up, and on the days I didn't have my daughter, I was in so much pain that I was doing whatever I could to escape (including a drug bender in Ibiza, which is really not as glamorous as it sounds; I had the worst comedown off ecstasy in my life there).

I started therapy with no intention of getting sober. I just knew that I had never felt so depressed or helpless in my life. I was a shell of myself, just a mess of blond hair and a Hermès belt with a belly full of wine and cocaine. Starting to talk about what I was feeling and knowing that I had someone to check in with weekly gave me just a little bit of stability when I needed it. For an hour a week, I began to see clearly through the haze of my addled mind.

On November 9, 2009, I took my last drink for almost a decade. My road to sobriety, finally, was just as dramatic as you might imagine. One evening, I was coming home from work on the 2 train when I had a

59

premonition. I can only explain it as divine intervention. I was standing up, holding on to the subway pole with my eyes open, and I had a vision of my family—my parents and my siblings, Sarah and Danny—all together, crying. I was dead. I saw Rob and Kier, and Kier was okay. It was a big loss, but she wouldn't really remember me enough to be devastated. I had seen my life without me in it, and it shook me to my core. I still don't know how to explain this vision; was it G-d? Because why would G-d give me a message and not speak so directly to others? Maybe it was something that I once heard described by a wise person as a Gift Of Desperation: G.O.D.

Whatever caused this epiphany, I knew then, in my gut, that if I didn't get sober, I wouldn't make it to my birthday that year. I called my friend Leslie, who is sober, and asked for help. To really own my problem felt like a big first step for me, and I'm so grateful it was received as such by Leslie. She was living in Argentina at the time but called one of her friends in the city, who took me to an AA meeting in the East Village.

That was the first step. My first meeting, followed by another, and then another. One day at time. At first, my body, mind, and spirit underwent the complete shock of withdrawal. I hung on even though I was fucking miserable. Two weeks into sobriety, I started to experience round-the-clock panic attacks. I lost so much weight that people thought I was sick. It was the physiological effects of withdrawal. I was missing the crutch I had used to cope for more than a decade, and now the pain of simply existing in my skin was too much. But I persevered. I went to meetings, and I stayed sober one day, one month, and one year at a time.

I didn't take a sip of alcohol for nine years after that. The first couple of years were a battle every day. There were always dinner parties, nights out with friends, celebrations, and, hell, even a hard Tuesday night, when I really wanted a drink. But I always knew that once I took that first drink, I would be totally powerless, and that knowledge alone stopped me in my tracks. The only way I have any type of control is if I don't take that first sip.

The beginning years of sobriety were hell, and I'm obviously not saying this to sway anyone from getting sober. It's worth it; it's just not easy. I cried a lot. I was consumed with guilt for not being fully present for Kier in the first years of her life. The old-timers at the meeting were the best. "Don't worry, kid, you're in the right place," they'd say. Along with, "Keep coming back," and the slightly strange but apt, "You're in pain because you're giving birth to yourself." I sat in the midnight group every night I could with the homeless, junkies, and insomniacs. I honestly felt so accepted there. I got a sponsor named Aggie, I worked the steps very slowly, and I started praying more regularly.

I kept going to meetings on and off for years. There were some things I liked about the meetings, and some things I didn't. But I went through all twelve steps, which I thought were amazing. I found it such an eye-opening, healing program.

I recognize the ways that I'm fortunate: my daughter's father is a truly good person and incredible parent. Rob is the best friend and co-parent I could ask for, and he has made having our daughter at a young age, and ultimately splitting, as graceful as possible. Around my one-year sobriety mark, we tried getting back together. I broke up with him when I was bottoming out, so when I got sober, I wondered if we should try again without alcohol as our third wheel. Rob agreed, and we tried— for us and, of course, for Kier. We booked a trip to Disney World with Kier in hopes it would kick-start our romantic energy; it's the most magical place on earth, after all. But on the trip, we both felt the lack of chemistry; even kissing was awkward and uncomfortable. We loved each other, but we couldn't consummate it. We'd missed our window.

I finally mourned our breakup and felt its full impact—I had been too fucked up to do it properly the first time. It was devastating to let go of that dream, but once I accepted it was truly over, I was set free from something I didn't even realize I'd been holding on to. The attempt at reconciliation changed the trajectory of our relationship and brought us closer. From that point forward, Rob and I have remained incredibly close friends, and we've known that we'll always love each other deeply, if not romantically.

As painful as the first few years of sobriety were, they were also filled with incredible gifts. Just being able to be present in my own life was the biggest of them all. I watched Kier as she turned three, and then four and five, with the wonder of a new parent. In many ways, it felt like I was seeing her for the first time. Maybe I was. I signed her up for ballet and other classes, and I went to every single one of them. I was a little bit of a helicopter parent, but I was making up for lost time. I look at photos from those years—which I took *so* many of—and I see the way she looks at me, like I'm her protector and hero. She didn't know what I'd been through or what I'd missed out on in her young life. She just loved me.

For Kier's third birthday, I baked twelve funfetti cupcakes with pink frosting and took them into her preschool class. I passed out the cupcakes to each child and we sang "Happy Birthday" before the kids dove into their treats. I looked around and marveled at the way each child enjoyed their cupcake so thoroughly. Some started from the top. Some took the paper off and ate from the bottom. Some just ate the frosting. Each child was beaming with innocence and joy.

Something came over me that morning as I hunched over in a tiny chair in that preschool on a small side street in the financial district. I realized the booze would have stolen that moment from me. But instead I got to marvel over the way these beautiful children enjoyed those cupcakes, something I still think about. I've spent the last decade thanking the universe for allowing me to be present.

Dead Inside

Along with the gifts of sobriety came the reality of sobriety. For years, every one of my underlying issues had been masked by the booze and whatever I could put up my nose. In the harsh light of day, my emotions were surfacing. I knew I needed more mental health support, and I was finally in a place to ask for it.

My therapist suggested I see a psychiatrist who specialized in addiction to help stabilize my system and manage my meds. I agreed wholeheartedly. After my first appointment with the addiction psychiatrist, I was put on an antianxiety medication, an antidepressant, and a stimulant. I went from illicit drugs to pharmaceuticals, but the effect was the same. I didn't know what my real emotions were; I could only feel what the medications allowed me to feel. And still, sometimes, that was too much.

I experienced bouts of depression during those first years of sobriety that were pretty unbearable. If you've ever had severe clinical depression—the kind of depression that has you thinking about the sound your body would make when it hits the pavement after you swan dive out of a window forty stories up—then you know exactly what I'm talking about. Sometimes, I actually felt nothing. I didn't want to die. I just wanted to be myself again.

The flip side of depression were those times when I became agitated and impulsive. I felt charming, seductive, and prettier. I was sexually insatiable, and I spent a lot of money I didn't have. Hypomania is a constant hunger, a constant need for stimulation, a constant thinking. Not hungry for food, though; I barely ate during those episodes. There's just no peace. No serenity. It's a state of needing more, nonstop.

The summer of 2012 had been filled with mood swings, but I never took notice of the up periods—only the depression, which came crashing down in the form of agoraphobia and total dread, plus the inability to get out of bed. After a few sessions with my addiction psychiatrist, one day he said that he'd been considering his notes again, and thinking about my waves of depression followed by periods of high energy. Sitting in my psychiatrist's office, on August 27, 2012—my thirtieth birthday—I was diagnosed with bipolar II disorder, a type of bipolar disorder characterized by depressive and hypomanic episodes, which means I'm manic-depressive. Happy fucking birthday to me!

And with that, out came the prescription pad to start drugging my psychosis. He started me on new medication that day, and that began a period of fighting doctors, fighting against labels and stigmas, and learning to advocate for myself. I was put on so many drugs, including heavy-duty antipsychotics, while still taking the antidepressants and antianxiety meds I'd already been prescribed. He even wanted to put me on lithium. I refused. Not because it's a hard-core drug, but because I heard it gives you pimples.

That night, my sister threw me a dinner at Mr. Chow in Tribeca, followed by a surprise birthday party at Macao. It was an amazing evening, but the whole night I was just trying to hold it together. I felt like I was having an out-of-body experience greeting everyone while also knowing I had gotten a diagnosis that day that would change me forever.

After the initial shock wore off, I accepted the diagnosis. Honestly, I felt a little relieved. I figured it explained a lot about how I was feeling as I swung wildly between the gravitational pulls of motionless depression and insatiable mania. At the same time, I was worried that I might not be able to get it under control.

Once I was diagnosed, I thought that things couldn't get much worse. Which means, of course, that they did. The medication my shrink put me on the day I turned thirty was bad. I became a zombie. The ability to feel anything was gone, almost overnight. My eyes were sunken, like my soul was just sucked out of me and wandering around separate from my body, lost somewhere.

But the worst part was the exhaustion. I couldn't keep my eyes open. If I mustered up the energy to actually take a shower in the morning, I would pass out again afterward. I can't even find the words to describe it. Again, Rob had to pick up a lot of slack during those months, and he did so with grace and respect for me and what I was going through. The guilt of not being able to function as a mom was the only thing that managed to break through the haze. It killed me. MTTM suffered immensely. I couldn't go into the office. Being creative was foreign at that point. I found myself sitting on the bathroom floor burning my arm with a cigarette, just to try to feel something. Who the fuck was I? I never did that type of self-harm. Ever. Not my thing. I was more prone to drink myself into oblivion and see if I woke up the next morning.

My psychiatrist kept upping my dosage, thinking it would help. At that point, I started to feel like I was losing my mind. I told my mom I needed to go to Bellevue Hospital, but instead she told me to get rid of the meds. My mom is a therapist, and although she doesn't prescribe medication, she has been seeing patients for over thirty years, many of whom were battling alcoholism and addiction. And she knows me. She watched me literally lose my life over seven months on the medication, and after watching me fall apart over other drugs as a teen, she knew when enough was enough. I threw out the bottle of pills and prayed my "self" would show up again. And—after a horrible period of withdrawal—it did. It was agony, but I prevailed.

Over the next year or so I was pretty stable. Until I wasn't.

Bitch, Interrupted

For a while, my life was defined by bursts of hypomania and depression. When I was manic, I'd make drastic moves, often without much consideration or warning.

Out of nowhere, I thought it would be a great idea to change Kier's school, buy a $10,000 couch, or be in a relationship with a married couple. I couldn't sit still, and I couldn't stop spending money. When the mania subsided, the 747 of depression would hit. BOOM. Once again I'd find myself sitting in my doctor's brown leather chair in tears. This time, I was worried about my mascara running because I'd decided I had a crush on my doctor.

When you're hypomanic, you don't want it to stop. There's no reason to ask for help. It's like a high without the drugs. During these episodes, I thrived professionally. I had the intense energy to create and go full steam ahead. Sales were up, and MTTM was doing better than it ever had before. I started a campaign I called "Bitchisms" and plastered posters all over downtown Manhattan with phrases like "Good Dick Will Imprison You," "Nice Guys Can't Fuck," and, of course, "Don't Be Scared to Be a Bitch." I would stand near them to watch people walk by, then stop in their tracks to take photos next to them. I was busy, traveling all over the world for work and for fun. I was social, staying out late, not needing much sleep. Still sober! I was on top of the world. The fact that this was possibly the hypomania part of manic depression never even crossed my mind.

Even though I was, on some level, thriving and productive, I wasn't well. Physically, my nervous system was shot. Even on the heavy meds like Seroquel, I was still a ball of nerves. Emotionally, I was reeling from an intense and destructive whirlwind romance. After spinning in my manic whirlwind for too long, I checked myself into Gracie Square Hospital—a mental health facility housed in New York–Presbyterian Hospital. I can say with full confidence that the decision changed my life.

The decision to go to Gracie Square wasn't a long-held plan. Once I realized that I did in fact need help, I packed a small bag and headed there immediately. I called Rob on my way to the hospital and told him what was going on, and then asked him to call my mom to fill her in. And, most importantly, not to mention anything to Kier, who was nine at the time.

Gracie Square Hospital is housed in an unassuming building on the Upper East Side, about a mile away from Sacred Heart. I checked in on October 5, 2016, and I spent a week in the psychiatric ward. When I arrived, I signed the paperwork and was shown to my single room. I felt relieved to hand over my phone, my ID, and my credit cards in exchange for a pair of hospital socks with rubber grips. I found a copy of Roxanne Gay's book *Bad Feminist* and lay down on my bed to read. I had such a sense of peace that I was in the right place to get the support I needed. I slept like a baby the first night.

The next day, it began to sink in that I was sitting in a psych ward in hospital socks and sweats. I felt like a failure. I was six years sober, and I thought that my life was supposed to have gotten better by now. I somehow managed to continue to create chaos, even without the booze or drugs. In fact, it felt like I'd replaced the booze and drugs with more sober chaos. I couldn't hide from myself anymore. I had to look in the mirror and see where I was at. I felt empty, fucked-up. My body felt like it weighed tons; meanwhile, I was about fifteen pounds under my normal weight. I just wanted to be myself again, so, so desperately.

I met with a new doctor, who reviewed my case and quickly took me off most of the medication I had been taking for several years. During our daily sessions, I felt heard and seen. I asked my doctor what I should tell Kiki to explain why she was staying with her dad. I wanted to lie and say that I went away for business, but he told me to tell the truth. So I told her a half-truth: that I was somewhere getting help for how tired I was. She was upset at first but cheered up by the end of the call.

I had to make the most of this—for me, and for Kier. I knew I had to get better, and I felt like I was finally taking care of myself and I felt cared for. Weirdly, I enjoyed getting my pulse and blood pressure taken by the nurses so often. We sat around most of the day, and I wasn't used to the quiet and the solitude. There were pay phones, which I would use often. I still have the sheet of paper with the phone numbers of the people closest to me who I would call. Friends came to visit and brought my favorite things (mostly juice from Juice Press). I didn't think about my love life. I didn't think about the brand. I just lived in the moment.

But when I looked around at the other patients, I often saw a stark difference between their struggles and my own. Some of them wrestled with delusions. Early one morning the woman in the next room began screaming—the most bloodcurdling, horrifying scream I had ever heard. It rang with a type of pain I didn't know. I passed by her room to look in and saw she was being administered a syringe of who knows what that helped her to quickly fall back asleep. I met a sweet gentleman on the floor, who I think was schizophrenic. He was so funny and loved Broadway musicals, so we would often sing songs from *Les Mis* together. One day he became so irate with the nurses that he shit all over his bed so they would have to clean it. The smell still haunts me. I could see that while I had my own share of problems to deal with, I was fortunate in a lot of ways. Maybe it was time to leave.

The problem is, once you're in a psychiatric hospital, it's not that easy to leave. But just like I did at New Hope,

I went to the director and told them I was self-admitted and if they didn't discharge me, there would be hell to pay. I packed up my hospital socks, returned my reading selections to the library, and off I went.

No one told me that one of the side effects of going cold turkey off one of the medications is a *very* increased sex drive that hits you all of a sudden. My mother drove me home from the hospital, and it was the most awkward drive of my life, because all I could think about was being horny. I actually ended up going back on Lexapro, eventually. I like having a dulled sex drive, and it does help my anxiety and depression so much.

In the hospital, I realized that I had to make better decisions for myself, because my mental health relied on it. Yes, I would always deal with some level of depression and anxiety, but I had the power to not put myself in situations that would exacerbate it. That was the most empowering realization. There was no one who could take care of my well-being except for me. I realized how fortunate I was, that I had the means and the ability to become healthier and happier. I had to own that responsibility and commit to it, which meant working harder to take care of my body and recognize my triggers. All of that effort is draining, and to be honest it kind of sucks to work so hard on yourself, because it can make you into a self-obsessed person. But I've learned what the alternative is the hard way, and it's a lot worse than being a little self-obsessed.

I also learned that relationships could be like drugs, and in the same way I couldn't stop using crystal meth or alcohol, I could become addicted to people. I realized that being in a toxic relationship, with its adrenaline-filled highs and punishing lows, completely undermined all my efforts to stabilize my mental health and stay sober. That realization may be why I've stayed single to this day.

The other important thing to come out of my hospital stay was the oversight of a new doctor who reviewed my medical history and determined that I did not need to be on heavy-duty meds. Ever since I stopped taking those meds and switched to other forms of coping, I haven't had symptoms of bipolar II—I am in remission, if that's what you want to call it. I haven't engaged in any hypersexual behavior, overspending, or other hypomanic behaviors. I haven't had depression so intense that it's prevented me from living my life. The pandemic was the one time since that I really struggled with depression, but I recognized that I was struggling and reached out to my doctor to change my dosage of Lexapro. I think the pandemic challenged a lot of us who deal with mental health issues. I'm always checking in with myself and evaluating how I feel. It's a daily thing. But I feel much more stable than I ever used to, even if I have off days or weeks. And I still see the psychiatrist whom I met at Gracie Square.

Sometimes I wonder if I really have bipolar II. The criteria used to diagnose me also happen to be the characteristics of someone who just doesn't know how to cope. If someone has bad coping skills, they might go on a shopping spree, or have a one-night stand, or find some other method of escapism. We all do that to some extent—that's why happy hour exists. But for those whose coping skills are poor, it can go overboard. For a while, I felt out of control, which is why I ended up in the hospital.

My mental health journey has taught me a lot—about my brain and myself. I learned never to let someone else label me, when I know who I am and what feels right in my gut. In addition to relying on my doctors, I also learned to advocate for myself. I don't blindly follow every suggestion; I ask the hard questions and do the research, too. (Note to readers: Please seek medical help if you need it, and don't take advice from a fashion designer, juvenile delinquent, and alcoholic.)

Sometimes I've wondered, *Why do I have this chemical imbalance, and who would I be without it?* Maybe all the drugs I did as a teenager fucked up my brain. Or maybe my brain was always like this. What I've come to realize is that no matter the reason, this intensity in my brain and body and being is what makes me who I am. And I love my intensity. I'm not for everyone, but I will never apologize for being myself.

CHAPTER 4
STRANGE ATTRACTORS

I've been more fortunate than many when it comes to relationships. It was sheer luck that I met Rob at such a young age—I can't imagine who I would be without him in my life. Or maybe it wasn't luck at all. Maybe it was fate, a collision course set by the universe to bring us together. There's no doubt in my mind that we were meant to crash into each other and never let go. In chaos theory, there's a philosophy of "strange attractors"—two points in a system whose behavior can't be predicted. They might crash into each other hard, intersect at various points, or never reconnect again. Somehow this feels like a fitting description of my romantic relationships (okay, almost all of my relationships).

I have been blessed to share parts of my life with

exceptional people—romantic partners, friends, business collaborators—who have challenged me and supported me in incredible ways, even if our encounters were brief. Aside from Kier, Rob is the most important person in my life. He's my best friend, lifelong partner, and, of course, my baby daddy. No one has taught me more than he has. He keeps me grounded while pushing me to be the best version of myself. He has made me a better person on every level—as a friend, as an entrepreneur and creative force, and definitely as a mother. I'm grateful I get to live my life with him by my side.

Soul Mates

Meeting Rob was one of the most significant moments of my life. I thank G-d every day that the laws of attraction brought us together. We met in 2002, when a friend invited me to check out this incredible streetwear store on Orchard Street called Alife. She had just started working there, and she knew they were hiring, so she encouraged me to come by. When I walked in, I immediately thought Alife was the coolest store in New York. They were working with artists, developing their own line of sneakers called Rite Foot, and featuring designs by obscure creators from around the world. It was a mixture of art and fashion, and the vibe was totally original.

I went up to the office on a second-floor loft overlooking the retail floor and met one of the owners, Rob. I said hello and asked about the potential job opening. Never one for professional pretenses, I had dressed like I normally did at that time: oversized parachute pants, a small, cropped tank with a bold logo, and door-knocker earrings. He was handsome, and looked me over with a sly smile as he said, "What are you, a homegirl?" It was silly, but I honestly fell in love with him on the spot. (And yes, back in 2002 you could say something like that to a stranger.) I didn't get the job, but I did meet someone who would become one of the most important people in my life.

A few weeks after I met him, my friend and I were going to one of DJ Max Glazer's parties at a club on the Bowery, and we walked in to see almost no one there except a couple of guys, including Rob. It was such a coincidence to run into him again after that first brief meeting, and I had to admit I was into him. It felt like fate. After we chatted for a bit, Rob asked for my number. I wasn't nervous about whether or not he'd call; I knew we were meant to be. He called the next day, and a week later, we had our first date. We met at a bar called Trailer Park on Twenty-Third Street between Seventh and Eighth

Avenues and then saw a movie on Forty-Second Street. We've been together in some form or another ever since.

On our second date, Rob took me to this hole-in-the-wall spot in Little Italy. Over spaghetti and meatballs, we talked and talked about our lives, our families, and our hopes for the future. He told me about his childhood, the way he felt about art and fashion, and what he wanted to name his kids one day. I loved the way he valued his family, and his calm presence felt like the grounding counterpoint I needed. We had so much in common, too: We both had a love for horror movies. We both grew up with Pekingese dogs. We both had intense mothers. I'll never forget how I felt that night—the wine, the candlelight, the way he was looking at me will stay with me forever.

Rob and I started dating when I was only twenty, and he was thirty-two. We fell in love and got serious quickly, and we stayed together throughout most of my twenties. I know I was young, but what we had was real love, not some juvenile infatuation. I wanted to be buried with that man—not next to him, but in the same coffin. We moved in together after three months of dating. I just started staying at his house and never left. Whether we walked around our neighborhood or grabbed drinks outside at Sweet & Vicious across the street from our apartment, or partied with the streetwear and artist circles we ran in—every day with Rob was exciting. He bought me Chanel for my birthdays and wrote me sweet letters. He was not the most expressive with his feelings verbally, but he was romantic when he wanted to be.

Rob and I often spent time with his parents, and we would go to Connecticut to visit mine. He was such a positive influence on my life. He kept me in check with a short leash, which I very much needed. My family loved him—dating Rob was probably the first good choice I'd made in my mom's eyes. There was something about him that just made me feel like I was home. And I hadn't felt like I had had a home in so long.

Rob was hugely inspirational for me professionally, too. He's so creative that it was contagious. He is the only original founder of Alife, and he was always the brand's visionary. His work was the intersection of art and streetwear, and he was doing it at the highest level. Alife had their own line, and also sold other people's brands. On top of that, Rob helped jump-start artists' careers. He comes from a graffiti background, and he curated art shows at Alife for artists like Dash Snow, Dan Colen, and Ryan McGinley. These guys are super famous now, of course, but were barely known at the time.

Rob was also an incredible businessman. He opened up the first specialty sneaker store where you had to buzz to get in. It's actually what motivated Nike to do this—

different-tiered sneaker levels where certain shoppers get a more exclusive selection and a specialized shopping experience. When Nike starts taking your ideas, you know you're doing something right.

People worshipped Rob's stores and came from all over the world to shop at them. I knew the kind of effect fashion could have on people, but Rob took T-shirts and sneakers to a whole new level. Like his collaboration with Levi's, for example. Rob worked with them to redo their whole flagship store into this sick art installation as they launched a new line of brightly colored denim.

While Rob was killing it, I just kept getting fired from every job or leaving because it wasn't working for me. I didn't know what I wanted to do. For a while, I thought maybe I could be a New York housewife. (I guess I did end up being one after all!) I could marry Rob, a successful business owner, have kids, and get my nails done. As if it's that straightforward. It's the exact opposite of what I ended up doing, but it definitely crossed my mind. I was struggling to find where I wanted to put my energy, and in that frustration, I looked for easy.

But Rob saw past that laziness and uncertainty. He always encouraged me to pursue my passions, and he showed me the work ethic that it takes to achieve your goals. My introduction to the streetwear world and my relationship with Rob started the wheels turning for my own creativity and desire to make a mark in fashion.

We had so many beautiful years, but it wasn't always perfect. Nothing is. Our romantic relationship eventually ran its course. After Kier was born, I thought he would propose, but he never did. There was something about the lack of effort or laid-back complacency that I'd once loved about Rob that was now irritating me. I thought, *If you can't even find the energy or interest to get a ring or propose, then you can't be my man.* There were obviously other issues at play in our relationship; as you know by now, I was drinking too much, and we had different priorities. At a certain point when I was spiraling in my own hurricane of mom guilt, addiction, and depression, I realized that I wasn't in love with him anymore. I knew that I couldn't stay in a relationship that didn't make me happy. I couldn't value the expectations of our families and community (everyone we knew was rooting for us to stay together) above my own desire for happiness. Ending things with Rob was really hard. And, yes, I felt like such a bitch for breaking his heart and tearing apart our family.

Right after the breakup, there was a lot of hurt, and anger, and sadness. It was a dark time. I'll never shake the image of little toddler Kier sitting on boxes when Rob moved out of our loft. She was heartbroken, and I felt like a villain. I tried my best to minimize her trauma as much as I could. I tried to make our new dynamic as positive as possible. I never spoke badly about Rob in front of Kier, even when she was young and might not understand, and I prioritized spending time together as a family as much as I could. Thankfully, Rob was on board. He put any hurt or resentment he felt toward me aside for Kier's sake. It was a little uncomfortable right after the breakup, but we both tried our best. Of course, there were times we fought and didn't talk for a few weeks here and there, but for the most part, it worked. We celebrated holidays together. We spent weekends taking Kier to the playground and out for lunch as a family.

When I met Rob, I felt like my life was complete. I thought I was never going to be with another man. I don't think I will ever experience a love like that again, which is a hard thing to come to terms with (I'm still working on it). I spent a few years after we split in a dark place, wondering if I'd made a mistake. I knew I wanted a different life—not necessarily better, just different from the one I felt we were heading toward.

For so long, I wondered, *Why do I love Rob so much if we can't be together?* It baffled me. But in sobriety, I've realized this is how things are meant to be. Our magnetism as a couple was brief but powerful, and our friendship and love going forward will last a lifetime.

Good Dick Will Imprison You

Eight months after Rob moved out, I decided to get sober. AA proved to be the most important tool in my sobriety, and, it turns out, sexually, too. After a month of sobriety, I started seeing this guy whom I met in an AA meeting, Jason. He was a total fuckup, but at least he was sober. He was an ex-rapper from Atlanta whose career was going nowhere. When Jason and I first had sex, it was my first real experience with sober sex. I had been fucked up for all of my sexual experiences since losing my virginity as a teenager—including with Rob. I had never had an orgasm from sex before Jason. For some reason, I felt more comfortable and open to trying things with Jason than I ever did before.

It's common in the twelve-step program to say that you shouldn't date within your first year of sobriety. I didn't heed that advice, of course. My relationship with Jason wasn't necessarily the healthiest, but I did learn a lot about sex and what I liked and didn't like. I learned to look someone in the eyes, even though it was terrifying at first. I learned to be communicative, to let my partner know what I did or didn't want. How else would he know? Jason was in my life for a very brief time, but it was an important time for me. It took practice to have sex sober and let go of my inhibitions and my critical inner voice, which was usually dulled by substances. (Sobriety made one-night stands an impossibility, too. I discovered I needed to have an actual mental connection and chemistry with a guy to enjoy sex—imagine!)

One of my strangest attractions was to an athlete I'll call Ted Bundy, and to say that we crashed hard would be an understatement. In the summer of 2016, I was in a manic state—sober, but struggling with medications, and swinging back and forth between debilitating depression and hypomania. Ted was gorgeous. Just being next to him made me gush like Niagara Falls. Even though he was hot, he was clearly bad news. He showed up wasted for our first date. He told me he was an alcoholic who would go on frequent benders. He had served a year in prison for drunk driving. Nothing could get between him and his booze. Knowing that addiction intimately, I made the only logical choice: I would save him!

We were doomed at first sight. We fell madly "in love" right away. A couple of months into dating, we got tattoos of each other's initials. The sex was off-the-hook insane—when he was sober enough to get it up. Things were a wreck from the start, but when they weren't and we had glimpses of normalcy, I swore that he was my soul mate. I was convinced my life depended on him getting sober. I was utterly obsessed with him and getting him off the bottle. In reality, I would've been better off shooting heroin than dating Ted. This isn't a blame game. I was a full and willing participant, and I signed on to have Ted fuck up my life. I kept going back for more. It's almost like I *wanted* to fuck things up, and I used him to do it. I could've walked away at any point—but I stayed. I went back, over and over, a glutton for chaos.

I thought it was a great idea when Ted suggested that we take a holiday to the Italian island of Ischia for our birthdays. (We're both Virgos.) He'd been booze-free for a month after the last bender, and I was hopeful this was the beginning of our life together.

Our Italian fairy tale turned into a nightmare reminiscent of an Italian horror film. After two days, I realized Ted was very, very drunk. I left him on the beach and walked alone around the little island crying, trying to call Rob and figure out what the fuck to do. I knew it was going to turn into a long bender, and I panicked, wondering how I would get home. Ted, meanwhile, stumbled back into our villa and proceeded to drunkenly say the meanest things anyone has ever said to me. I told him I was going home, and he threw a laptop at my head. Luckily, I ducked in time, so it smashed against a wall and not against my eye as he stormed around the villa screaming that he was going to kill me. This was it.

I went home without Ted. He ended up staying in

Italy in a blackout drunken stupor, and his family had to go there and bring him back to the States, from what I heard afterward. I spent the next month in a daze. I felt dead inside. Heartbroken. Defeated. And I felt like I really needed some help.

My relationship with Ted was one of the final straws that pushed me to check myself into Gracie Square, so sometimes things happen for a reason. I haven't been in a serious relationship since then, and I don't know if I ever will be. It's certainly not something I'm actively seeking. Dating is such a clusterfuck of games and pretenses, and I'm not interested in wasting my time on it. I've just seen too many gorgeous, smart, successful women caught up in whether or not a guy was texting them back. In some ways, dating has never been easier with all of the apps, social media, and ways to connect. And yet, because people make snap judgments about whether to swipe in a matter of seconds, it's never been harder to be yourself. You're going to have to be yourself at some point. It might as well be from the beginning.

Even though I'm very open about my stance on dating and my needs, people still don't believe me. Well-meaning friends will tell me that I'll change my mind when I meet the right person or that I should just put myself out there anyway. And maybe they're right. Or maybe I have everything I need at the moment: a beautiful daughter, a supportive and loving co-parent in Rob, and the ability to date and have sex when I want to. Maybe I don't need or want more than that.

Heart Full of Love

Of course, romantic relationships haven't been the only tricky ones in my life. I realized at the ripe age of thirty-nine that it was time to work on my relationship with my mom. I'm trying to take ownership of my behavior and accept her for the wonderful—but still flawed—human being she is. For a while, I was caught in a dynamic with her that was based on our old behaviors—it's like our relationship was frozen in time. We actually seemed to connect over my bad behavior. I like to tell her everything—or almost everything, and certainly more than most people tell their mothers—but I hadn't stopped to consider that maybe she wants less information. We are both fully formed adults, and I don't think either of us is planning to change. Still, I am trying to be kinder and more compassionate. I have not cursed at or told my mom off in a year. That's huge progress.

My grandmother's death was a huge turning point in my relationship with my mom. I remember walking into my grandmother's bedroom one afternoon, and seeing my mom sitting at her bedside, crying. She was speaking to her mother, telling her how much she would miss her and how she didn't want to live without her. I knelt down by my mom and just held her. In that moment, my mom looked like a little girl, reaching out for her mother's hand. I saw her in a very different light. She wasn't the tough, all-knowing presence I'd always seen. My mom doesn't ever show vulnerability, so seeing her in such an emotional state impacted me a lot. We often don't think of our parents as human, until something happens that's big enough to break down their superhero facade.

That moment with my mom and my grandmother—and the fact that those were my last moments with my grandmother—kind of changed everything. I knew that I had to treat my mother with much more respect. I knew that I had to stop blaming her for shit and stop fighting with her. That wasn't what my grandmother wanted when she passed. If I don't want to run around in circles with her forever, I have to change the way that I act and react. It might be late, but better late than never.

If I'm being honest, my mom probably has some PTSD from my teenage years, too. I was not easy on my parents, and I think she's still carrying around some of the tough love and hard exterior she had to create to parent me at a time when I was so self-destructive.

Take, for example, that time when I was sixteen years old and I had ordered a taxi to take me to the bus station. I was on my way into the city for a night of drinking, dancing, and whatever else I could find at a club. My parents had other ideas. When I tried to leave to get my taxi, they barricaded the front door. After years of drinking and drug use, and one rehab stint, they wouldn't let me out of the house. I knew that in Connecticut, you're considered an adult at age sixteen. So I called the cops and told them that my parents were holding me hostage in my house. The police came and told my parents that they had to let me go. I will never forget the look on my father's face. He looked totally defeated and exhausted. I felt a pang of guilt, but quickly moved on. I had a club to go to, after all. My mom followed me out and was physically trying to drag me back into our home. The taxi pulled up across the street at the $2 movie theater to pick me up, and my mom begged the driver to leave without me, gripping my jacket. I was yelling at her to let me go and to stop ruining my life. Of course, all she was doing was just trying to keep me alive for another night.

I felt like there was no sympathy for me as I battled my addictions. I was treated like I was a bad person, and it made me even angrier and made me want to get fucked up even more. I really just wanted my mom to give me a hug, to hold me while I figured it all out. I told her that once, and she said, "How could I ever bring myself to hug you with the way you were acting?" I guess she was right. I remember my parents joined a tough-love group to help them deal with me. I saw the pamphlet on the kitchen counter, and I fucking lost it. I told them they didn't need a group to teach them tough love!

While it may have felt like my mother was holding me to an impossible standard, the bar was actually very low. She simply wanted me to finish high school and not be a drug addict. And yet, I felt intense pressure from her to be someone I couldn't be at the time. I blamed her for a lot of my struggles. I see that now, after many years of conflict—a lot of love, as well, but so much conflict. I know I dragged her into my chaos during those wild teenage years. All the hard decisions she made—like not allowing me to live at home—damaged me, but there were two other, younger kids to consider. I know that as much as she wanted to protect me, she also wanted to protect them, and she couldn't do that with drug dealers showing up to the front door, threatening her. For so long, I felt like even though I worked hard to make something of myself, she was disappointed in me for not living the life she wanted me to live. It just wasn't fair. But now we're at a place where we still bicker and have our moments, but we've also accepted each other.

My dad and I have had our share of struggles, too. In high school, we spent an entire year not speaking. I would walk through the house and go upstairs to my room, and he wouldn't look at me, let alone talk to me. It felt terrible, and I numbed that pain with more drugs. I don't know that hugging and empathy would have made me any less of a drug addict, but I do know that's what I wanted at the time.

Once, when I was on ecstasy, I wrote a letter to my dad. I told him how special it was to me that we were close when I was a kid. I reminisced over all of the things we used to do together, like ride the Staten Island Ferry, or take trips to Coney Island, or even ride between the subway train cars—a dangerous but exhilarating experience. My dad and I were so close when I was a kid, and I wanted us to get back to that place. I left it for him to read, and I went to hang out at my friend's house. My mom called me there and said that whatever I wrote in the letter really touched him, because he was crying. Things changed a lot after that.

Today, my relationship with my dad is great. After almost dying from a brain aneurysm years ago, my dad awoke from a two-week coma with a new zest for life. Even though his health issues can sometimes physically limit him, he has such a positive attitude. He loves to throw back cocktails and listen to Green Day. He's a fun time!

Raising my daughter has given me a different perspective into my parents' experience of raising me, and I've gained a newfound respect for them. It's fucking hard being a parent! I've realized that every decision they made, even if I didn't like it or think it was the right choice at the time, was made with the absolute best of intentions. Just like I do with Kier. It's important to me to be very tapped into what's going on with her. Right now, our communication is great, and I hope it stays that way for the teenage years ahead. We have a closeness and a friendship that I didn't have with my mom, but that I always yearned for. Maybe it skips a generation, because my daughter and my mom have an amazing relationship. Bunny calls my daughter every day, and I wouldn't want it any other way. She has helped me raise Kiki, and she's been an incredible influence on her. They've forged their own close bond that's separate from my relationship with my mom.

Thankfully, too, Kier is a different person than I am. She is so much smarter, so much more in touch with herself and level-headed at fourteen years old than I was. Still, a taxi driver once told me that if your teenager doesn't hate you, you're not doing a good job of parenting, and I think there's some truth to that. It's about respect and setting limits as much as it's about being an open door to listen and give advice. Of course, she could

very well end up on a shrink's couch blaming all her issues on me, too. If that does happen, I'll tell her, "When
you're a mother one day, you'll understand."

So, yes, count me among the millions of people with
"mommy issues" who whine to their shrinks at $200 an
hour about how their moms didn't love them the right
way. It has taken a lot of years (and a lot of therapy) to
see that we are all human and flawed and bullshitting
our way through—even my mother.

The Siblings McSweeney

My parents aren't the only family members who suffered because of my tumultuous youth. I'm very lucky
that after everything I put them through my siblings
are still talking to me. It wasn't easy to grow up with
my bullshit overpowering the family and eclipsing their
needs, and I feel very bad about what my brother and
sister had to deal with.

There are so many crazy stories that they've since
told me—many of which I have no memory of. Like the
time they were woken up in the middle of the night and
brought over to a neighbor's house so that my parents
could get me out of the hospital after I almost overdosed.
Then there was the family vacation to Florida. That's

one I do remember, at least mostly—but their perspective was a lot different from mine.

We made the almost twenty-hour drive all smushed together in my parents' white Dodge minivan. My mom and dad took turns driving, and we sat in the back seat eating peanut butter and jelly sandwiches they had packed (no McDonald's for the McSweeney family!). When we arrived in Cocoa Beach, I realized we were a mere five hours from Miami—where a gorgeous guy I had been talking to in the city happened to be on vacation. I thought this was the perfect opportunity to meet up with him. Granted, five hours isn't exactly a reasonable distance for an evening out, but I was eighteen. I bought a ticket for a Greyhound bus, and I promised my parents I'd be back the next day. I said that I was visiting a girlfriend and that we were going to a concert.

Instead, I commenced a weeklong bender with this guy. Within an hour of getting off the bus we were having sex in the ocean at Nikki Beach. I swallowed a handful of Vicodin and chased it with champagne. We spent the whole week drinking, taking pills, doing blow, having insane sex. I don't remember much, but I definitely got into a fistfight at a nightclub. And I remember waking up on a lounge chair at a pool with no idea how I got there. Suffice to say, my little stunt pretty much ruined the McSweeney vacation.

I feel bad for causing so much drama in my family. It could never be about Sarah or Daniel because I always made it about me. Sarah was angry and resentful toward me for a while growing up. And I get it. We've done a lot of healing since then—thank G-d. When she was about sixteen, she started to understand the pressures and challenges of being a teenager (especially a teenager with our parents), and we were able to connect in a new way. Little by little, we've worked through our issues and become closer. We're in a great place now, and she's such a huge and important part of my life. I'm close with my brother, too, who's nine years younger than me. He's super smart and a deep thinker, which makes him very sensitive to the world. He's served as the mediator in my family many times. My mom listens to him a little more than she does the rest of us.

If there's anything I've learned during the isolation of COVID, it's that the people in our lives are more important than anything else. I'm going to keep working on my relationship with my mom and try to see my family as much as possible. I cherish my fleeting time with my now high-school-aged daughter. We like to take long walks around the neighborhood together, talking and window shopping. Whenever she wants to discuss the inner workings of her school's social scene, I put down everything I'm doing and give her my full attention.

I know the days of understanding the dynamics of her friendships are limited. I try to cook for her as much as I can. I've noticed the way she responds to a home-cooked meal instead of takeout, even if it's just spaghetti. The food isn't great, but I can tell there's something so comforting to her when I make dinner for us and we eat at home together. These are the moments that matter most.

And I've made it a goal to reach out to my friends more often, to find ways to meet up in small groups and appreciate one another's company. This year for my birthday I didn't throw an over-the-top party or plan a big group night out. Instead, I focused on small dinner parties, so I could spend time really catching up with my close friends. It might sound simple, but it's so meaningful. After all, what is our life without the people we love?

CHAPTER 5
BODY IN MOTION

They say there's a rule that a body in motion stays in motion—and that's one rule I do seem to follow. In my early twenties living in New York, I saw the evolving styles that a new generation of clothing designers brought to the table. Once I had more exposure to streetwear and the downtown art scene, I was hooked. I loved the irreverent, bold graphics, and the fusion of other styles, including athletics, skate, and hip-hop, to create something entirely new. I wanted to learn everything I could from Rob and his circle, so I spent hours at Alife and the other big shops in the city, observing, absorbing, and hanging out with the innovators pushing boundaries.

During that decade, trends changed, and the old relics

of streetwear from the '90s, like Ecko Unltd., Phat Farm, and Triple Five Soul, were on their way out, which made space for the new brands like Alife, Supreme, SSUR, and A New York Thing to find success. I quickly noticed that these brands didn't offer women's lines, and there were few female voices in streetwear. So I took matters into my own hands. I bought men's clothing and tailored the pieces to fit me in more figure-flattering silhouettes. I bought oversized T-shirts with dope logos and daring designs, then cut and tied the fabric to create my own style. I loved making something for myself that no one else could have, and I started to gain some respect from Rob and his friends for my fashion sense. I knew there had to be other women like me who struggled to find brands that catered to them. I began to formulate the idea of designing a streetwear line for women.

Recently, real estate legend Barbara Corcoran told me that the business I ended up creating wasn't a model a typical entrepreneur would follow because it was too risky. I guess there's just something inside me that laughs at the thought of what can't be done. So if you feel like the people around you misunderstand your vision, don't allow yourself to be deterred. Often truly creative people— and I mean those sick fucking geniuses who change the culture and blow open the restraints of "how things are done"—don't fit into our reality. They have their own way of seeing the world. Imagine if Warhol or Picasso, Kanye West or Lil' Kim, listened to the critics and naysayers around them. We wouldn't have the incredible innovations that have changed our culture. In my own arena, I've created something different from what existed before. And it's taken me a long time to have the confidence to say that.

Downtown Dreams

I turned twenty years old in 2002, and with the entry into my twenties, I felt a renewed sense of self. Yes, I was still drinking too much and partying too hard, but I was back in New York and I was finally finding a place where I fit in. Through friends, I started hanging out with graffiti artists, musicians, designers, and artists who were part of a vibrant downtown scene. I went to these incredible rooftop parties, bars, and gallery openings where I would meet so many interesting, creative, often out-there people. One night, I met a few graffiti artists, including Adrian Moeller, who owned a magazine called *Mass Appeal*. It was a legit magazine with smart and defiant features on music and culture and killer streetwear fashion spreads. I begged him to let me intern there. I loved the creativity of visual storytelling that I'd studied over all those years of devouring *Vogue*, and I was intrigued by the fashion content at *Mass Appeal*. I wanted to learn more.

After pleading my case to Adrian and promising I would work hard despite my party-girl reputation, he agreed. I interned at his magazine for a couple of months, during which time the fashion director, Jill, took me under her wing and gave me real insight into photo shoots and styling . . . which I was able to observe from behind a giant pile of clothes I'd been asked to steam or boxes of props I'd been asked to move, pack, unpack, and sort. It was a lot of bitch work, but I was just excited to be there.

At *Mass Appeal*, I got a primer on the streetwear scene, and I saw firsthand that business was booming. The new generation of streetwear designers were becoming celebrities in their own right, getting invited to trade shows and parties by international fashion media. I was so inspired by their glamorous trips around the world. They were doing what they loved—innovating and rebelling against the status quo—*and* living the life.

During this time, I also worked part-time at Satellite Records, one of the few record shops in the '90s where you could buy tickets to raves and casually run into Junior Vasquez shopping. It was a real rave mecca in 2001, and I was soaking up the fashion, the music, and the vibes in the epicenter of the culture. Satellite was owned by the legendary Scott Richmond, and it was run exactly how you would imagine. We were all party animals. We would regularly find baggies of drugs that would fall out of customers' pockets and do them in the bathroom, praying it wasn't heroin.

Scott was trying to help us all like he was the father of a dysfunctional family. One day, he invited me to lunch down the street at Time Café and told me he saw something special in me and wanted to help me. He offered to pay for me to go to the Landmark Forum, a self-help and "personal development" organization that I always thought was a little suspicious. My response was, "Hell no! I'm not going to a cult! I don't have issues!" Whether it's a worthy program or not didn't matter to me. I wasn't trying to do *anything* self-help related back then. I wanted to relish in my new independence, and I felt that I had helped myself plenty already. I wish I hadn't been so judgmental about the program without trying it. Who knows? I might have learned something.

After a few months assisting the fashion director at *Mass Appeal,* I decided to reach out to a few stylists for my next internship. I was bold, and I had no problem emailing or cold calling to ask for work. I was never afraid of rejection; I expected it, actually. So imagine my surprise and excitement when someone responded positively. I had more opportunities in fashion styling than anyone I knew, and I had zero connections and minimal experience. Sure, I wasn't getting paid (a luxury you can afford when you're living rent-free with your grandma), but I was learning so much.

I worked with stylist Rebecca Weinberg—the former wife of *Sex and the City*'s famous costume designer, Patricia Field—on and off for a few months. After that, a friend of mine hooked me up with an agency that needed an assistant stylist for a magazine photoshoot with actress Marcia Gay Harden. The shoot was at the Soho Grand Hotel, and when I met Marcia and her then husband, Thaddaeus, who was the photographer, they were both so kind and cool. As I chatted with them they complimented my outfit and asked me a million questions about growing up in New York. I could tell the stylist I was assisting was getting annoyed—she straight up treated me like Cinderella, ordering me to steam hundreds of pieces of clothing we would never use. When Marcia and Thaddaeus invited me to drinks after the shoot, my boss unloaded another list of tasks to prevent me from joining them. I did everything she asked, and then I quit the styling assistant business.

So, yes, you could say I started my career in fashion at the ground level. I went from living in a halfway house and working retail to living with my grandmother and working unpaid internships. But there's no position too low if you're chasing your dream. When people ask me for professional advice (it happens, occasionally!), I always say it's important to be humble and do the things you may not want to do if they get you closer to your goal. I steamed the clothes and I picked up the coffees, all while soaking up the knowledge around me. But after that day on set at the Soho Grand, I hit my limit. I was back to square one, trying to figure out what I was good at and what was compatible with my lifestyle. Because let's be real, the biggest obstacle I faced in the workforce was just showing up. I was not cut out for the early mornings of corporate life, to say nothing of my aversion to rules and authority. I kicked back and waited for inspiration to strike.

Married to the Mob

I became friends with Rob's best friend's girlfriend's sister—which, yes, sounds crazy. Sharon was a cool Irish chick from Yonkers, who worked in finance and had impeccable taste in clothes (she turned me on to Goyard and Balenciaga). We hung out all the time, partying and wreaking havoc. One day we were sitting on my stoop on Spring Street, where Rob and I lived, drinking to-go margaritas that we used to get from this Mexican restaurant around the corner. Those were the best days, in our twenties, with no worries and barely any hangovers. That day, margarita in hand, I thought back on my idea to design streetwear for women. I turned to Sharon and said, "I want to start a clothing line. Let's fucking start one!" She took a long sip of her margarita before smiling. "Hell yes!" We both knew all of these guys with clothing lines, and we saw them traveling all over the place for free, making great money, and commanding a lot of respect. I told her about how I'd been altering men's clothing for years, and we agreed that we needed to do it.

We sat on that stoop for hours, long after the sun went down and our margaritas ran dry. We talked about the kinds of designs and brands we loved and what we hoped to achieve. I felt the electric rush of a good idea. I had always joked that the girls in our group were "married to the mob" because all we did was go to brunch and have drinks while our men worked. Suddenly we had the name of our business: Married to the Mob. Of course, there's nothing less realistic than a twentysomething with no job or direction comparing herself to a mob wife, but at least I had a healthy sense of self. One of our first designs was a T-shirt with the phrase "Bitches Who Booze" instead of "Ladies Who Lunch," a riff on that origin story.

I wasted no time getting started. That night, I made Rob sit at the computer as I directed him to design a T-shirt collection, which consisted of four graphics. I hovered over him, and we played one of my favorite Lil' Kim songs, "Queen Bitch." In it, she raps: "Queen bitch, supreme bitch." Supreme is the name of a major street-wear brand, and I thought it would be cool to use a play on their logo for the graphic for "Supreme Bitch," with white blocky letters on a red stripe background. That original Supreme design is actually based on the work of artist Barbara Kruger.

The next morning, I took the design to Alife and asked one of the guys, Ricky, who had just bought a screen printing machine, to make the T-shirts. He graciously agreed, and I went to Friedman's wholesale T-shirt place on the Lower East Side to pick up some American Apparel T-shirts in white, black, pink, and kelly green. Armed with the shirts, Ricky took my designs and printed the first fifty. Now, all I had to do was sell them.

My first stop was Union, a store on Spring Street that featured a curated selection of streetwear brands. It was owned by James Jebbia, the founder of Supreme, and his ex-girlfriend Mary Ann, who ran the store's operations. I had known her for a while because I shopped and hung out there. I took the T-shirts to her, and she loved them. On the spot, she took them to James to see if he approved of Union selling them—especially touchy since I used their logo for the design. He was in! She took a bunch to sell on consignment, and they sold out in a few days. Once my T-shirts were in Union, we were in business. Everyone looked to Union to set the trends. We sold through the first run of T-shirts, and I was contacted by other stores that wanted to place orders.

We quickly built a website for Married to the Mob with a design inspired by the Chanel site. Orders were coming in from streetwear stores all over the city and the world, and we continued to expand printing and create new designs. The graphics were designed by Rob with my creative direction. We were a great team. My aesthetic with his skill and expertise. Two of my most popular T-shirts from the early collections were brightly colored designs with irreverent sayings. The first featured the pink, green, and yellow text of "Boys Ain't Shit but Hoes & Tricks," and the second said, "My Girls Rock Balenciaga & Smoke Mad Marijuana." I also did a T-shirt featuring a photo of my "money manicure," which entailed pieces of cut-up dollar bills affixed to my nails. The photo went viral and was used in so many MySpace backgrounds it became notorious. But the "Supreme Bitch" design was the cornerstone of our first collection, and it came to define the brand early on. It put us on the map.

I officially launched Married to the Mob in the sum-

mer of 2004 when I was twenty-two years old. I had no in-
vestors, no wealthy parents, and no one to open the doors
and pave the way. I did have a front-row seat to Rob's master class in hard work, unyielding ambition, and creativity combined with entrepreneurship. It was bound to rub
off eventually! I learned an important lesson: When you
surround yourself with people who inspire you, you get
better. I hadn't done a lot of that in my life, but hanging
out with Rob and his crowd pushed me to up my game.

Initially, MTTM was really just a fun challenge. I
never imagined it would have any longevity. I started
a business with $4,000, almost all of which was used to
pay for materials and printing. But after about a year,
I realized it was working, and the brand was real. Unfortunately, my business model of buying bulk T-shirts,
printing them, and selling them to stores by hand wasn't
exactly high margin, so I didn't have the cash to scale
the business. I was happy to be getting some traction,
but I had no idea how to get to the next level.

Put Your Money Where Your Mouth Is

Then, a bizarre but fortuitous incident came back into play.
Three years prior, on July Fourth, 2001, I was physically

assaulted by a cop outside of Hammerstein Ballroom, a music venue in the city. I had gone to an EDM concert, courtesy of free tickets from my job at Satellite. At around four thirty A.M., all the concertgoers flooded out of the venue and onto the streets, where we were met by dozens of cops. I had run into an old flame that night, and we left Hammerstein holding hands, blissfully unaware of the mayhem that was about to ensue.

I was kissing the old flame goodbye when I felt him being pushed away from me. I opened my eyes and panicked when I realized he was being pummeled by several NYPD officers who were beating on him with their hands and batons. Without hesitation or much thought, I threw my half-empty mini Poland Spring bottle in the direction of the chaos. Before I could process what was happening, I saw the bottle hit one of the cops in the back. He turned around, and we locked eyes. I froze. I knew what was going to happen next. I will never forget the look in his eyes as he lunged at me and swung with a closed fist at my face. He punched me so hard that I spun and did a 180 before falling onto the ground. The impact of my fall knocked the shoes from my feet.

The lower part of my body lay on the sidewalk, while the upper part of me landed on the subway grates of Thirty-Fourth Street and Eighth Avenue's northwest corner. I felt knees on my back and my hands quickly pulled behind me and wrestled into handcuffs. My half ponytail was now in one of the officers' hands in a tight grip while he slammed my face into the metal grates and said in a growl, "That's what happens when you fuck with me, you little bitch."

I was in shock. I wasn't crying or screaming. I was numb. I was finally pulled to my feet and that's when I realized I was barefoot. As I started to register my surroundings, I saw that all the customers in the Tick Tock Diner on the corner were plastered to the windows, staring at the scene unfolding in front of them. I often recall this story with a lot of levity, but being physically assaulted by the police—a group of imposing men—was traumatic, and it still impacts me. Trauma lives in your body and becomes a part of you.

As the police assaulted me, bystanders were screaming at them to stop. I could hear people yelling, "Get off of her!" and "That's a girl you're beating up!" A few people called 911. In New York City, when 911 is alerted about a police officer possibly committing a crime, the Civilian Complaint Review Board is notified, and I was contacted by them the next day. I had one year to formally press charges for the assault, and it took me almost that long to bring myself to do it. I was still kind of terrified, and the last thing I wanted was to see that cop again. But just before the statute of limitations ran out, I found a lawyer. I sued the NYPD for one million dollars and, ultimately, received a $75,000 settlement. I invested every penny into my company. I was able to quit my retail job, put all my time into the brand, and buy my first computer. Of course, I also went to Barneys and bought two Goyard bags. But then I felt guilty and returned one.

That is the definition of putting your money where your mouth is. I was young and broke, living with my boyfriend, and that money could have been spent or snorted so many ways. But I had a vision for a successful business, and I wouldn't let anything deter my ambition. I had to put everything I had into realizing my dreams. I worked plenty of nights and weekends in the process of scaling the brand. It was all-consuming, but I had finally found my "thing," and I loved it. MTTM started to get attention from established fashion media—including my beloved *Vogue*, a totally full-circle moment for me— and soon we began turning a healthy profit. Rob and I moved into a beautiful loft apartment with the help of my paycheck. I remember looking around our giant new place, feeling pretty damn validated that I had done things my own way. For me, success was never a sure thing—and that made it even sweeter.

A Style Like No Other

To go from a teenager devouring *Vogue* and worshipping Deee-Lite singer Lady Miss Kier to a successful streetwear designer was literally a dream come true. Even when I felt lost and low, fashion was my tether to the world. Growing up in New York, I was surrounded by street style. Chelsea in the '90s was a very vibrant neighborhood, with an anything-goes attitude, and I was totally inspired by the freedom and creativity around me. I had a front-row seat to incredible styles and sartorial trends like nowhere else in the world. I lived a few blocks away from the iconic clubs Limelight and Tunnel, and at nine years old, I would watch the club kids before I even knew what club kids were, their platform sneakers so high they could barely walk down the block. There were also a lot of sex workers in my neighborhood, and they were always dressed to the nines. I'll never forget when I saw a woman wearing a red thong, teddy, see-through bra, and heels, holding a matching red umbrella. I thought she looked powerful, so much so that the image has stayed with me twenty-five years later.

In eighth grade, I babysat for the fashion editor of *Seventeen* magazine, Amy, which gave me another perspective into the fashion world. Her husband was a photographer, and they lived in one of the nicest buildings in

Chelsea, a few blocks away from my family's apartment. I had these very '90s, A-line short skirts in different pastel colors, which I bought because they reminded me of a Versace ad that featured Claudia Schiffer, Naomi Campbell, and Christy Turlington all wearing coordinating metallic pastel skirts. I wore my miniskirts to babysit a lot, which is admittedly not the most childcare-friendly choice, but Amy complimented my looks frequently, and that was certainly worth it. Sometimes she would ask where I bought my accessories or outfits, or what color my lip gloss was, and the next thing I knew my favorite shops and brands were being recommended in *Seventeen*. It was pretty validating to feel like my finger was on the pulse of what was cool and a magazine editor was recognizing my taste.

Amy invited me to a fashion show at Bryant Park Fashion Week one September. It must have been 1995, or around then. Bijou Phillips was walking the runway. I was able to bring my best friend, Jennifer, and I dressed up wearing heels, one of those pastel skirts I loved so much, and a see-through top with a black bra. I felt like I had arrived.

When I was growing up in the '90s, I loved brands like Baby Phat, Betsey Johnson, and Anna Sui. I shopped at Antique Boutique, JackThreads, X-girl, and Liquid

Sky. I loved mixing the styles I would find at these stores with, say, fake Versace sunglasses with the big gold emblem on the side, and a pair of Nike Air Max or Airwalk sneakers. One piece I loved from JackThreads was a halter top that was made from Star Wars bedding, which just barely covered my boobs. I paired that with huge jeans. I was obsessed with Liquid Sky, a record label and ubiquitous rave clothing store that was *the* place to shop and boasted Chloë Sevigny working the register. Chloë Sevigny was the downtown alt-scene It girl, and she seemed to be forging her career as a model and actress on her own terms with her own unique sense of style.

While I loved the glamor of a fashion show and all of the luxury brands, the high-end scene has never truly been my thing, and I coveted the downtown street style. When I needed to get a dress for a formal dance in eighth grade, I dragged my mom to Patricia Field's on Eighth Street in the Village. Every other girl in my class was going to Bergdorf's, but Pat Field's store was a favorite among musicians, club kids, and stylists. I found a long, iridescent purple dress with spaghetti straps that I loved. It was the perfect form-fitting style, understated in its cut and loud in its fabric and color. I was trying to sell my mom on it when a group of drag queens shopping nearby chimed in. With their support, we convinced my mom (who thought it was too revealing). I still have the dress, and I wore it to a charity event recently. Thankfully, I was a voluptuous eighth grader.

In the late '90s and early aughts, the fashion world was hip and edgy and unafraid in a way that it's just not now. I was obsessed with the way Lil' Kim and Gwen Stefani used to dress. Lil' Kim is undoubtedly one of the biggest style icons of all time. She took risks with outrageous ensembles and bold colors, and I loved the way she combined the provocative with luxury designer logos. Like a fur coat, string bikini, and a Gucci belt. Gwen had a very different West Coast look, but she also dressed to her own beat as she rocked a mix of eclectic styles: the androgynous, not overly feminine vibe; and the streak of fuck-you rebellion that seemed to seep out of her pores. They both experimented, pushed boundaries, and never followed anyone else's rules.

It was also the era of teenage girls ripping fashion ads out of magazines and taping them in their school lockers or on their bedroom walls. It was such a peak time of fashion advertising. Some of the ads I remember most vividly featured sex, drugs, and nudity in innovative, creative ways. There was a Sisley ad by Terry Richardson with two girls snorting lines of cocaine that morphed into a white dress, promoting their "Fashion Junkie" line, a Tom Ford Gucci ad where the model's pubes were shaved into a "G." And let's not forget the Calvin Klein ads featuring hot, young models in their (tight, suggestive) underwear. They were *so* sexually charged.

I took a lot of inspiration from all of these different influences—from the club kids and flamboyant queens of Chelsea, to the Upper East Side princesses, to the sexy shoots of the advertising industry—to create my own evolving aesthetic. New York is the kind of place where ideas are all around you, and street style was about riffing on these inspirations and innovating. In the city that never sleeps, the turnover of ideas and styles is constant.

Time to Level Up

As MTTM grew, opportunities to collaborate with established brands began to come my way. I was introduced to someone at Nike, and he seemed interested in how we might work together. I played my full-court press: I took this guy out, got him drunk, and dragged him to karaoke in Chinatown. The rest is history.

I designed an athletic shoe with Nike, a Nike Dunk SB, based on a Chanel tweed pump. I wanted to create a visual nod to their signature toe cap, and I used patent leather to create a similarly inspired look. This was a *huge* moment for MTTM. I also worked on designs for a track jacket and a T-shirt with the MTTM logo right next to Nike's. It's still incredibly special to me that Nike wanted to use my logo alongside theirs—sharing space with the swoosh is a big deal.

When you're working with a giant company like Nike, you obviously have to sign off on a lot of paperwork, including waivers that state you own every little mark of your brand. When I reviewed the papers before the collab launched, I realized that I didn't own the trademark for "MOB," just for "Married to the Mob." The folks at Nike were understandably pissed, and truthfully, their trust in me was probably a little rattled. We had to drop the track jacket, but we were still able to release the T-shirt and the shoes. We held a release party at 12 Mercer, and I was able to take a step back and really appreciate the fruits of my labor.

The creative direction behind the photo shoots and the marketing of MTTM has always been my passion. I love having the ability to tell a story visually and share a point of view through a combination of clothes, styling, sets, and props. *That's* why people love fashion—it's such a powerful mode of expression, a way to show the world who you are and what you're about. You might not think of a T-shirt or a jacket or a bikini as a demonstration of identity, but it's all wrapped up in how we present ourselves to the world. So naturally, right off the bat, I threw myself into directing our photo shoots.

For my second collaboration, with KAWS in June 2006, I designed a limited-edition bikini in a black-and-gold snake print. The photographer for the shoot, Lynette, had a friend in her building who owned a giant albino python snake. Lynette asked him if we could shoot in his apartment with his snake, and he agreed.

So off we went to the Bronx for a photo shoot with a snake. My operations manager, Lourdes, kept a box cutter handy just in case the snake attacked us—or, more likely the model, who happened to be my sister, Sarah. (I know how owners are with their pets. They'll let a person get killed before they kill the pet.) We were terrified, but we got some amazing photos. I'm happy to say that the box cutter was never used on the snake or anyone else. Sometimes it's all about taking chances. And I'm glad Sarah was willing to take a chance!

There's No Such Thing as a Mistake

I'm learning—through trial and error, many stumbles, and some outright failures—that there is no right way to live your life. I become stronger through adversity. I become smarter after every misstep. When you let go of the fear of making mistakes and disappointing people (including yourself) or being wrong or embarrassed or failing, you're free to be confidently, fearlessly *you*. In my professional life, I tend not to listen to industry "rules" and instead find my own way. Sure, I've fucked up, but those are the lessons that have helped me the most. I also don't take advice easily, which I'm sure doesn't surprise anyone.

In 2012, I designed foam trucker hats with "Supreme Bitch" in big, bold letters. (Don't come for me about the trucker hats; 2012 was a very different time, and trucker hats were a thing.) When I received the boxes of merchandise from the manufacturer, I was disappointed by the quality. The fabric and the finishing weren't exactly what I had specified, and the result wasn't at the level I expected. But they also weren't a total mess. I knew going back to redo them would delay my orders by months— and I had a lot of orders to fulfill.

At the time there were five interns at Mob, and when it came time to ship the orders, they approached me together and asked to talk. They said they were disappointed that we were shipping merchandise that didn't meet our quality standard. The nerve! I told them I had a business to run and the hats were fine, but the truth was, their concern fueled my own. I wanted to stand by every single item with certainty that it was the very best and the very highest quality possible—I still do. So I started to question my decision. Did I make a huge mistake? In the end, I stuck to my guns; this was about more than the stitching on some trucker hats; I was the leader of a company that employed other people. I needed to send out product and get those receivables to keep the business afloat.

A week later, the paparazzi snapped a photo of Rihanna wearing the "Supreme Bitch" hat on a yacht. The next thing I knew, our hat was all over the internet . . . and MTTM blew up! It was a critical lesson for me in trusting myself and standing by my decisions as a businesswoman. I had started to second-guess myself, in part because others thought I was making a mistake. But I followed my gut, and the results proved me right.

My instincts to move back to the city and figure myself out led me to the life I have today. Within two years of moving back, I had met Rob and infiltrated the streetwear scene. There were a lot of errors in judgment and just plain drug-fueled bad behavior that led me to that halfway house in the city, but still, they put me on the path to be exactly where I needed to be. I'm not the sum total of every bad thing that has ever happened to me. Through many years of therapy and working the program, I finally understand this.

If I had been allowed to live at home after rehab, I might have stayed in Connecticut forever and continued drinking and partying, instead of moving back to the city and being forced to make it on my own. In fact, I may not be alive today if I'd followed another path.

If I'd never met Ted, I wouldn't have ended up in Gracie Square Hospital, and then I wouldn't have received the medical attention I so desperately needed. As a result, I got off the meds that were crushing me.

If I hadn't started drinking again after nine years of sobriety, I wouldn't have ended up seeking a stronger spiritual community, which led me to convert to Judaism.

These have been some of the hardest moments I've experienced. But they have also been the moments that have changed the course of my life in meaningful ways.

I have been knocked down and sent back to square one, believe me. But I kept going, smarter and stronger each time. That's my ego dragging my sorry ass up out of the gutter to make something of myself. It's hard to have an ego when you're living in a halfway house. Ego isn't all bad, though. It's what makes us brave and reckless—both key ingredients to getting shit done and being a badass.

When You Least Expect It

I've learned over time that there's nothing more important than who you are when your back is against the wall. The grit and resilience you have in those moments—or don't—is the difference between success and survival—and not. Sometimes it just takes action to find the way out of a bad situation. Fighting the paralyzing fear and the inertia to stay in motion is the first and hardest hurdle to overcome.

The road to near destruction of my company was paved with bottles of wine, lines of coke, and too many excuses and distractions. The year 2015 was a fucked-up one for me. I lost myself in a toxic relationship (see: Ted, Chapter 4), and Married to the Mob was going down the drain. I had been so absorbed by my own bullshit that the brand really suffered, and I was about to pay a real-life price.

I remember vividly a conversation with my accountant in late November of that year in which he told me that I needed to reduce our staff. When I asked how many people he recommended, he replied, "Everyone, Leah." Sales were slowing down dramatically, not because we didn't have stores to sell to and not because we weren't relevant but because I had neglected my company. I fucked up. I pretty much skipped a season of sales, and it screwed up my cash flow. We had nothing to sell, and the expenses and bills were piling up. It was a dark time for me, and I couldn't stop thinking, *How the fuck could I let this happen?* I felt like such a failure.

I didn't know what to do to right the ship, and my energy was focused on beating myself up instead of working toward a solution. I listened to my accountant and started letting people go, some of whom had been with me since the early days. Telling my dear friends that I was letting them go right before the holidays gutted me. One of them was so pissed she didn't speak to me for a year. It was a somber month, and most of the time I didn't show up to work. I never want to disappoint people, especially the people I love.

I was struggling mentally and felt so beaten down that I resigned myself to closing shop. I remember sitting in my Dumbo office all alone. The desks were empty, strewn with handwritten to-do lists that would never have their items crossed off. Racks of clothing lined the walls. The office—once filled with so much buzzing, laughter, visitors in and out, photo shoots, and meetings—was eerily quiet. I told the landlord I didn't need the space anymore, and he agreed to let me out of the lease. I told him I'd leave after Christmas.

In early January, I attended an annual event in Colorado for a store I worked with called Zumiez. Brands flew in from all over the world, and Zumiez would bring in pro skaters and random celebrities (Dennis Rodman showed up once). I knew it would be the last one I would attend. I didn't tell anyone that, but I went to take it all in and say goodbye. As I was leaving a party at the lodge, I ran into the son of one of Canada's biggest streetwear licensing guys. I hadn't seen him in years, but I remembered him and his family. By some stroke of luck, he asked me if I was looking for help with MTTM. *Actually, yes, I am.* Just like that, I was back in the game.

I still can't comprehend that just when I thought I was down and out for good, I met the right person to help me turn the company around. It goes to show that you never know what will happen. I was ready to accept the fact that MTTM was closing. I even interviewed with Adidas for a creative job, which thankfully I didn't get. I had started to imagine a life where I commuted to Portland for the workweek and came home on weekends to be with Kier. I really didn't know what I was going to do. But it was clear that I loved fashion, and this is where I belonged and what I was meant to be doing.

Never Stop Evolving

I've accomplished one goal in my life with Married to the Mob, and recently, I felt inspired to take on a new professional challenge. I started a sustainable sleep-wear line called Happy Place, which has proven to be an incredible creative and business opportunity for me. Launching a clothing brand this time around—with almost twenty years of experience under my belt—is a whole different experience. I'm smarter, savvier, and have an infrastructure in place around me, which means I'm no longer spending hours packing boxes with my interns.

Creatively, working on a sleepwear line involves de-signing for a different set of needs in my customers' lives. I created the collection in different colorways than MTTM; instead of bright, bold colors that capture the energy and dynamism of streetwear, I chose soothing earth tones for Happy Place. The line is also all fully sustainable, which was a goal of mine from the outset. The clothing industry creates a lot of waste, and I've been a part of that supply chain for a long time. With this business, I wanted to challenge myself to do better for the environment. Our sleepwear is all made with or-ganic cotton, the water that's used in the factory and in all of our packaging is recycled, the factory itself is solar powered, and the cotton farmers and factory employees are paid a fair wage. I'm proud of what we've accom-plished in a short amount of time—we've already added baby blankets and additional fabric offerings for the robes—and look forward to expanding our line further.

Who knows what's next? I've surprised myself so many times over the years that even I'm excited to see what the future holds. Nothing annoys me more than complacency. How can you accept the status quo? I try not to spin my wheels in pointless motion for the sake of it, but rather find challenges that will really fulfill me. I listen to my gut when it comes to deciding where to invest my energy. Sometimes it swings more toward work, then other times I'm pulled to spend more time at home with Kier, or with friends and family. Time attending to my well-being. And then my gut may swing me back toward working like crazy. We're only here for a short time, after all, and I want to make the most of it.

CHAPTER 6
PREDICTABLE AF

If you would have asked me, even three years ago, if I could picture myself in a cocktail dress holding an apple on the set of a Bravo reality show, I would have told you to lay off the nose candy. It wasn't exactly where I thought I'd be at thirty-seven, but when the opportunity to join the cast of *RHONY* presented itself, I decided to go for it. If nothing else, I knew becoming a Real Housewife would push me out of my comfort zone—and I've certainly never been one to get too comfortable.

The experience of being a Housewife is the true embodiment of chaos theory. You might think the show is predictable—several women from successful backgrounds flitting around Manhattan, the Hamptons, or tropical resorts—but let me tell you, it is anything but formulaic. These women are the most unpredictable wild cards I've ever dealt with, and that's what makes filming with them insane in the best possible way. They've taught me lessons I didn't know I needed to learn, a strange combination of toughening me up and breaking me down. They make my life look tame by comparison, and that's coming from a girl who got eighty-sixed from almost every club below Fourteenth Street, including the debauched Max Fish.

The year leading up to my first season on the show was such a peaceful time in my life. I was experiencing the kind of calm and quiet that had always eluded me. At twelve, Kier was mostly self-sufficient, not to mention incredibly funny and strangely wise beyond her years. She was a pleasure to spend time with, and I found myself slipping into a version of motherhood I really loved. It was less about the physical work of lugging around a toddler, or constantly yelling "be careful" to a small child, and more about showing Kier the world. Nothing made me happier than when she enjoyed my favorite dish at a restaurant, or became obsessed with an old movie or song that I'd played to death as a teenager. Rob, Kier, and I were having a lot of fun, and it was feeling good.

I had been sober for nine years, and while it was never truly easy, I had more or less reached a place of equilibrium, a truce with my demon, if you will. I didn't look too far down into the abyss while I stood on the edge, and the demon never reached up to pull me down.

Married to the Mob celebrated its fifteenth anniversary at the end of 2019—even though I mistakenly celebrated that anniversary a year later on *RHONY*. I felt comfortable with my place in the streetwear community, and I was enjoying a sense of accomplishment that we had stayed in business for so long and found some success. I couldn't believe it when I would occasionally come across women on the street wearing our original designs. They were practically vintage!

So what does a chaos junkie like me do at a time like this? She fucks it all up! I couldn't stay in this kind of contented, drama-free life for too long. Sometimes I felt like I was crawling out of my skin.

It's All Under Control

The road back to booze was a slippery one. By my ninth year of sobriety, I felt really in control, and I started to wonder if I could have an occasional glass of wine or cocktail when out to dinner or celebrating something.

I was invited to Shabbat dinner at a friend's house in Battery Park. I had become friendly with Blake, the mom of one of Kier's friends, and over the years I had gotten to know her and her four great kids. Kiki and I loved being included in their Shabbat traditions and joined their family from time to time. Blake is an excellent cook and makes everything you could want for a Shabbat feast, from homemade hummus to a delicious lemon chicken dish.

When I went into her kitchen one evening, I noticed that Blake was drinking a Bloody Mary with Tito's vodka, which I thought was an odd choice for a Friday night. She told me she has one drink a week, her favorite Bloody Mary, while cooking Shabbat dinner. It's become a beautiful ritual and celebration for her. I thought to myself, *G-d, that's so nice. Maybe I can drink that way.* I was tempted to have a drink for the first time in a long time.

Later, when we were all seated for dinner, we passed the traditional kiddush cup of wine around the table, and when it got to me, I took a sip. My daughter looked at me, shocked, and whispered, *What are you doing?* I told her I was just being respectful during Shabbat. But honestly, that sip of alcohol changed everything in my brain.

It's not like that one sip of wine sent me on a bender that night, but it pushed me a little closer to the edge. I couldn't help but look down into the abyss as I started to think about drinking more and more.

A few weeks later, Kier and I went to LA to visit my sister, Sarah, who had just given birth to a baby girl. She was living out there with her fiancé. One evening, Sarah was on the phone drinking a glass of red wine, and I just grabbed the glass out of her hand, much to her surprise. I said, "Watch this," and I chugged the whole thing. She watched me with her mouth open in disbelief. She had experienced the ramifications of my teenage benders more than anyone, and yet when she was old enough, we became partners in crime. I set the glass down and felt the warm rush of the wine make its way through my body. I felt that green light of addiction click on, and it felt so good. It felt like an itch that hadn't been scratched, and now I was weak from the relief.

I really don't know what came over me in that moment, except that maybe the thought of drinking had been sitting in the back of my mind, lurking, ever since that Shabbat. Something about watching Sarah sip her glass of wine was just that one push I needed to tip over the edge, swan diving into G-d knows what.

When I got home from LA, it was off to the races. I stopped going to my twelve-step meetings, which I'd still been attending sporadically at the end of my sobriety, and I started going to the liquor store. I'd have an occasional cocktail or glass of wine at the end of the day or with dinner, and it was really nice. I felt in control every time I poured that glass of wine. No thoughts of finishing the bottle, no desire to chase a glass of wine with anything stronger. It was the summer, and I spent a lot of weekends going out to the Hamptons with Rob and Kiki, and some of our close friends. It felt so normal and adult to enjoy a glass of wine with everyone at dinner.

I began to think I wasn't like all of the other alcoholics. It must have been a phase for me, albeit a long one. But now, I had solved my alcoholism, and I was cured. I felt so proud of myself for being able to "handle my liquor," finally! After dinner, we would go out for the night, and I would have maybe three drinks—a seemingly reasonable amount of alcohol, no more than anyone else was having. After not drinking for so long, my tolerance was low, and the buzz would hit me in just the right way. I could still have a good time with my friends without getting wasted. I really believed I had it all under control.

Real Housewifey Material

My entrée to *The Real Housewives of New York City* came when I was newly off the wagon and navigating the very tricky footing of drinking without disappearing for a week in a Brooklyn warehouse rave. I wasn't completely losing it, but I was getting close. There would be one night out of five when I would just let go. I'd have as many glasses of wine as I wanted at dinner, which turned into shots and cocktails at a bar, which turned into lines of coke at someone's apartment. Suffice to say, I was in a pretty precarious state to have cameras following me constantly.

The opportunity to do the show came about the same way I get all the best intel in New York: through my facialist. She works on the faces of many celebrity clients, including one Ms. Bethenny Frankel. As it goes every season—when the producers are looking for new blood, the women on the show suggest other women in their circles, either ladies they know from afar or personal friends. Bethenny had been following me on Instagram and she wanted to give my name to the casting people. She asked our facialist to feel me out to see if I was interested. I was flattered that she thought of me, especially because we didn't know each other personally. I figured, why the hell not! I gave my facialist the green light to pass along to Bethenny, and we got back to my caviar-green-tea facial. Anything for good skin, am I right?

Shortly after that, a Bravo producer slid into my DMs on Instagram, and a week later she brought a camera crew to my apartment to film a short interview. I was determined to be myself, not to slip into saying what

I thought she would want to hear. If I was going to do something this out-of-the-box, I wanted to do it authentically. It was a fairly casual conversation in which she asked me about my life and my thoughts on the show. In response to one of her questions, I remember saying, "I'm not a socialite, I'm *anti*-socialite." And then I waited.

I got the call from Lisa Shannon, the VP of development, telling me that I was on the show while I was walking home from a friend's apartment after one of my first benders since falling off the wagon. If that wasn't an omen, I don't know what is. Still, I was thrilled to hear the news. Shocked, too. I had been myself and pulled no punches, and they wanted me. It was an incredible, if possibly crazy, opportunity.

Then, I did what I always do: I got in my damn head about it. I had a different perspective than many of the women on *RHONY*, and coming in as the "new girl" was intimidating. This group of women was known for their larger-than-life personalities, and while I hadn't watched *RHONY* religiously, I had watched the *Real Housewives of New Jersey* and I knew all about the blowout fights, the drunken escapades, and the way that rumors made their way into the tabloids. I knew I could hold my own. But it still felt *big*.

I was terrified about just what a huge responsibility it was to be on television, and how it would undoubtedly lead to me having my life—and the lives of my family—scrutinized. All of my mistakes would now be open for public consumption and judgment. Every word I said would be analyzed and dissected. Was it really worth it? I could second-guess myself right out of this opportunity, or I could rely on my instincts and take a leap. Every time my mind played through the scenarios, I came to the same realization: There was no way of knowing unless I tried.

Thriving in the Lion's Den

When we started taping the show, I felt like I was at Sacred Heart all over again. The Upper East Side setting was the same, and the group of women was worldly and wealthy, fretting over who had what and who was gossiping about whom. I was left wondering where I fit in among them.

My first day of filming took place at Dorinda's end-of-summer party, where I would meet the women for the first time. I told myself I wasn't going to drink that night as a conscious decision. I was in such a slippery place with my alcoholism after spending the last few months dabbling with drinking. Some days I could keep it in check with a few drinks, but once in a while, I would totally go overboard. I didn't know if drinking that evening would calm my nerves and get me out of my head, or if it would push me over the edge into being belligerent. The only thing I knew for sure was that I didn't want to make my drinking (or not drinking) a big attraction on the show. I worried that I couldn't control my drinking the way I wanted to in such a new, high-pressure situation with cameras following me everywhere. But it wouldn't matter. The beast was unleashed, and the idea that I still had any control over it was an illusion.

At Dorinda's party, I got mic'd up, and the producers literally pushed me into the scene for Tinsley to introduce me. It was comforting to have Tinsley there—we had developed a real friendship by that point, and I felt like she had my back. When I met Tinsley, I didn't know what to expect. Our initial conversation started out as small talk, about New York, comparing stories on past boyfriends and the best colorists for blondes. But, to my surprise and delight, she was smart, vulnerable, funny, and a hell of a good time. She opened up and told me about her fall from grace and her arrest in Palm Beach, and I told her about my own experience getting arrested. Over martinis, we compared our mug shots. She was deeper than I'd imagined, and we became very close very quickly.

When we arrived at the party—with lights and mic

checks, and cameras following us—Tinsley and I made a beeline for the bar. I was faced with my first on-camera decision to drink, or not, within ten minutes of taping. I ordered a Red Bull, and I desperately hoped the cameras wouldn't focus on my order, but then of course, Tinsley made a big deal of not toasting with me because I didn't have alcohol in my drink. So much for flying under the radar. I knew I would have to address the issue on camera soon.

Meeting Luann, Ramona, Dorinda, and Sonja was pretty intimidating. I immediately felt their critical gaze from under their false lashes. Sonja did a full up-and-down visual scan when we arrived at the party, like she was taking stock of my body and my outfit. I shook their hands, one by one, and introduced myself with a big nervous smile. I felt sort of out of my body at first. I was quieter than I usually am as I stood back and took it all in for a minute.

Becoming a Real Housewife was something I never could have predicted, and yet within a couple of hours of filming, I started to feel comfortable. I loosened up as I fell into conversation with Luann (another gal with a mug shot!), and I recognized who these ladies were— women wavering between confidence and self-doubt; party girls who loved to spend their evenings hanging from chandeliers and flirting with men; and, ultimately, savvy AF business moguls who were making a name and a brand for themselves.

That first night gave me a glimpse into the Real Housewives drama up close and personal. Okay, it wasn't quite that bad, but I did see Dorinda and Tinsley get into a heated argument. At first, I was shocked. I watched them yell at each other with my mouth open for a while, as if I was part of the audience at home. I didn't know if I should laugh at how absurd their argument was, or get involved and defend my only friend in the group. I'm never one to pull punches or to let people walk all over me, or my friends. It seemed fun to use "I may float like a butterfly, but I sting like a bitch" as one of my *RHONY* taglines, but it's absolutely a truth that I live by. Still, I was pretty tame that night, for me.

There were several other moments that evening when I found myself speechless as I took in the action around me, including when a drag queen began performing Luann's "Feelin' Jovani" song. Luann and the ladies sang and danced along. I had heard the song before, but I couldn't force myself to dance along to it; I didn't have it in me to fake it. So I stood to the side, quietly sipping my Red Bull. Maybe it wasn't the best way to make friends, but I didn't care. And with that, my inaugural night as a Housewife was in the books!

The truth is that as uncomfortable as the show has

made me at times, it's also pushed me to grow. I've definitely learned a thing or two, and often those experiences have been humbling. I've also had to know my own mind and defend my position in ways that have honed my communication skills and solidified my beliefs.

For example, there was the time when my mental health struggles became the target of gossip. When we went to Mexico on a group trip, I found out that Ramona had discussed my bipolar disorder and what medications I was taking on camera. I was disturbed that she would think it was okay to talk about my medical history so cavalierly with the cameras rolling—not to mention that her knowledge of my mental health was based on an article I had written several years prior.

I knew I had to confront her about it, and even though I was incredibly hurt and offended, I was able to stay calm and get my point across. It was one of the few times that I wasn't so triggered that I was screaming. I told Ramona that it wasn't her place to bring up my medical history and that I was shocked that she would gossip about something so serious. I said that she should have come to me directly if she had questions or concerns, but to bring it up to the group was unacceptable. I wanted her to know that I worked really hard to get through that time in my life, and I was in a healthy place. It's completely wrong and inappropriate to talk about someone's mental illness and presumed medication regimen behind their back. Suggesting that I was mixing my meds with alcohol and that's what made me act "crazy" is a pretty vicious accusation. She was trying to suggest that my bipolar diagnosis was responsible for my drunken antics, which is simply not accurate. In fact, this is a common issue for people dealing with mental health issues—anytime you have an emotional reaction or make a mistake, people blame your mental illness immediately. But we've all seen Housewives lose control after too many drinks—without being judged or shamed about the state of their mental health.

While I felt good about the way I handled some situations, when I watched my first season back on TV, it wasn't all gratifying moments. I also saw myself regress to "high school Leah." I wasn't always proud of the way I acted or responded to certain triggers, but once it was captured on camera, I had no choice but to sit with the discomfort and learn from it. I could either spiral into shame or embarrassment, or I could see it as an opportunity to move past that old baggage. It was like I had been given a second chance to work through my bullshit. The ways that I had felt like an outsider at Sacred Heart resurfaced as I navigated Upper East Side society for a second time—it was definitely a triggering environment for me. Now, with the wisdom and perspective of adulthood, I could finally see my way through it. Talk about karmic fate.

I didn't need to carry around the past experiences of being expelled from school, of sometimes wondering if I fit in among my high-society classmates. The reality is I fit in everywhere I went because I am myself. If you continue to tell yourself a story about yourself, you're going to believe it, even when it's not true. These limiting beliefs don't serve us; they keep us stuck in a cycle. I needed to evolve and break out of my rut, and seeing my behavior reflected back to me on the screen was the greatest first step. I realized that I have plenty to offer. I wouldn't let these ladies make me feel small—and I wouldn't make myself feel that way, either.

Too Much Is Never Enough

I quickly learned that I could be myself on camera and get a rise out of the ladies. I began to enjoy making them laugh, or pushing their buttons by talking about sex or other provocative subjects. I was having some fun with it, and adding another element to their already booze-laden, chaotic energy. But their energy fed my own energy, and before long, I was losing control too often.

One particular episode of the show, titled "Hurricane

Leah," followed a group trip to Rhode Island, and I hit a pretty raw moment as I struggled to handle my drinking and my emotions. If you've seen the show at all—or basically any promo reel for the season—you might remember seeing me drunk, writhing around on the ground under a dinner table yelling at Ramona. At one point, after a few martinis, I had gotten so worked up about wanting to have Sarah join us on the trip that I just lost it. I walked around the table with a boot in one hand and a shattered martini glass in the other, with one foot kicking at the camera.

I watched the screener a few days before the episode aired. I was newly sober again—a decision I made after losing control one too many times while filming, and which was now confirmed as I watched myself black out on-screen. I felt so vulnerable knowing the world would see this. Of course, I also knew it would make for great TV. When the episode aired, the media compared me to a Tasmanian devil because I was such an intense windstorm of emotions. And it was true! I was simultaneously trying to handle a grueling new work schedule and being filmed most of the time, which is the most unnatural, intense thing ever, alongside trying to manage my alcoholism.

The trip to Newport took a toll on my relationships with my castmates. It was hard to know where the line was with them. Some booze-fueled brawls and late-night antics were received with delight, while other escapades generated biting criticism and drama. After that trip, I wanted to cool it both with drinking and with stirring up the shit on camera. I pride myself on owning my mistakes and knowing when to make amends. It was similar to how I felt the morning after our infamous night at Ramona's home in the Hamptons, where I threw the tiki torches across her yard. I knew that I was in the wrong, that we'd made a big mess during our drunk shenanigans. When I woke up, the first thing I did was clean up and apologize.

But immediately upon our return from Newport—before I had a chance to make peace with them—Ramona and Sonja reached out to Bravo and told show execs they were concerned about me. They said my behavior had scared them. For some reason, I was scary as a blackout drunk, unlike the other women who get wasted and wild on the show. To Bravo's credit, they took this concern seriously and handled it in the most supportive way. They had a psychiatrist reach out to me, which I actually appreciated. It was nice to talk about how I was coping on the show with someone who was familiar with the pressures and objectives.

While it wasn't clear if Ramona and Sonja's "concerns" were about my well-being or their own, I did, thankfully, have a supportive circle of friends who had my back throughout this process. They've always been my conscience and my mirror when I lost control, and when I started filming *RHONY*, I leaned on them even more. My best friend, Jackie, said that she was very worried about me after the MTTM anniversary party that aired at the end of my first season. It's funny, because that party was one of the best nights of my life. It was merging the last fifteen years—MTTM and my longtime streetwear friends—with the show and new friends. I had the best fucking night, and it wasn't just because I was drinking. Having all of those people from different parts of my life there, celebrating and socializing together, was just amazing. It's how I imagine people feel at their wedding reception—a room full of everyone you love there to support you is pretty fucking great, regardless of the occasion. I saw Luann, in her sequined dress and fur shawl, chatting with Kunle, aka Earsnot, the notorious graffiti artist of the IRAK crew. And Sonja talking to my longtime friend Robin—whom I met when I was pregnant with Kier almost fifteen years ago—then screaming at me during my speech to make sure I gave Robin a shout-out.

I *definitely* had a few drinks at the party, and the

cameras were rolling, but it could have been so much sloppier. I was drinking too much, too quickly, and as I ordered another drink, I evaded the cameras like a true stealth addict. I knew it wasn't a good look for me, or for Bravo. Jackie was trying to keep me in check and, at the very least, help me not make a scene on camera like I was capable of doing in that state. She told me the show could either be about me being a train wreck or about me being a smart businesswoman, but not both.

This wasn't an isolated incident for me. Things would escalate almost every time I drank, which is basically why I no longer drink. Jackie knew that the show was going to provide access to a lot of parties and opportunities, and she didn't want me out in the public eye being sloppy once I became recognizable. She said, "People are going to give you whatever you want. You need to be careful." It's not always easy for someone to give me advice, so I was grateful for her concern.

I feel super lucky to have friends who have my back no matter what—who help me find my Chanel bag after losing it while blackout drunk—and friends who love my daughter like their own. They defend me fiercely and look out for me tirelessly. My friends challenge me and keep me in check. They don't sugarcoat; they call me on my bullshit even when I ignore them and dive into the deep end of mayhem, like when I dated Ted against their vehement warnings. Or when my friend Sherry picked me up from my recent plastic surgery, and she surveyed my bandages and said, "I hope this was worth it!" It totally was.

This may be morbid, but I measure the value of my life by how many people would attend my funeral. And honey, it would be jam-packed! I am so lucky to have so many people in my life whom I cherish and who cherish me. I pride myself on how I have maintained and held on to meaningful relationships for decades. I'm rich in people who love me.

Reality TV Is Not for the Faint of Heart

I think it's fair to say that I'm a little different from the other members of the *RHONY* cast. During my first season on the show, I brought more of a downtown energy to the Upper East Side (I don't think any of the ladies had seen Lil' Kim's face on a dress before I showed up). I knew I wasn't there because of my luxurious penthouse apartment, or because I would throw a lavish soiree with the upper crust of Manhattan. It was very freeing to go into the situation without the pressure of being someone I'm not. So it wasn't all that surprising when they had a strong reaction to my over-all vibe and appearance. Like the time I was having lunch with Sonja and Tinsley, and Sonja made some judgmental comments about people who have tattoos. It was such a thoughtless thing to say. I reminded her that some of her favorite musicians have tattoos, as do the designers she wears and loves. It was just such a ridiculous and out-of-touch observation that I couldn't muster the energy to be outraged. I corrected her and moved on.

I also felt judged by Luann when she came to visit me when I was sick one day. It was nice of her to bring me soup, but her reaction to my cozy, converted two-bedroom apartment in the Financial District was un-deniably negative. I don't know what she expected, but I could feel her judgment the second she walked in. At first, I thought she might be acting for the show, but be-lieve me, it was real. She seemed to hesitate before she would even sit down on my humble couch.

Opening up my home to cameras obviously impacted my family's privacy, and when I first agreed to join the cast, I was worried about how the exposure would impact them. I sat down with Kier and Rob, and we discussed the pros and cons, and the reality of what it would be like to receive more attention. We educated Kier on what to expect as best as we could, and she seemed comfortable with it. She's really taken the changes and the exposure in stride. Ultimately, I think it's a positive thing for both of us. But I'm always keeping tabs on Kier and how she's handling it. I'm continuing to reevaluate the effects of the show on our family, as I do with most things.

Reality television is a unique way to enter the celebrity realm because when viewers get an inside peek at your life, they start to feel as though they truly know you. There's a sense of intimacy from people who stop me on the street or say hello at a restaurant that sometimes takes me aback. It's very different from the experiences I had with celebrity culture when I was growing up. I didn't know Gwen Stefani and Lil' Kim personally, but I appreciated their music, their style, and their take on the world around them. It was a fandom built out of respect and admiration at a distance. When people know you from reality TV—and even more so from social media—fans often feel their relationship with you is based on a real knowledge of who you are and a shared sense of community. Social media facilitates true connection, yes, but it also enables a kind of communication that's invasive and unhealthy (telling a recovering alcoholic that she's "more fun to watch" when she's drunk, for example, is a pretty cruel comment to make).

In the boundaryless (and often anonymous) world of social media, "fans" also have no qualms about calling someone out. It's exhausting and stressful to have thousands of strangers scrutinize your every move, your every outfit, your every choice, down to the color of your lip gloss. And if you're not careful, all of that noise can start to chip away at your sense of self. Everyone is entitled to their opinion, of course. But when thousands and thousands of opinions (read: thinly or not-so-thinly veiled insults) are coming at you regularly, it can be overwhelming.

I get so many comments on Instagram about the clothes I wear on the show. I truly don't care what people think of my style; I'm having fun, expressing myself, and adding a little edge to the show. I don't need the approval of the masses to feel good about what I'm wearing. And the same is true for MTTM designs; they're not for everyone. I've got Rihanna wearing Mob. Enough said, right? When Rihanna posted a photo of herself in one of my T-shirts, I felt a huge sense of vindication and relief. I can wholeheartedly say that once she publicly defended me, I haven't paid even a morsel of attention to nasty Instagram comments or tabloids. It was the reminder I needed that Married to the Mob isn't for everyone, that I'm not for everyone, and that I should focus on the opinions of the people I respect (like Rihanna, obviously).

That's not to say I've been perfect. There have been a few incidents that have made the tabloids and created a little drama. Nothing I'm proud of and nothing I'm worried about. I don't spend any more time than necessary on low-life, energy-sucking people who want to tear me down and stir things up for a little time in the spotlight. It's not worth it to me, and I'm not interested in those power games.

That said, one recent tabloid headline really got under my skin. My publicist sent me the article, and I was appalled. It was completely false and so obvious that the publication was trying to jump on the bandwagon of public interest. There was a part of me that wanted to send a cease and desist and go nuclear, but I calmed down and realized that it wouldn't be worth it. I swallowed the urge to respond in any way, like tweet out how terrible this magazine is, because I knew it would give the fake news more attention. I just won't ever participate in another interview for this magazine, which, I think, is a healthy response that shows where I stand and reinforces my boundaries. Sometimes I say, "Not today, Satan." Other times, I clap back.

All of us will have experiences where others will try

to beat us down. People may say bad things about you or spread untruths. I've been judged for my clothes, my tattoos, my education, my hair color, and my attitude. When I'm criticized by others, I don't retreat into my shell. I get angry. I work hard to prove them wrong in my own way. You might not feel that same anger, or it might be rooted in a different emotion—but whatever you tap into, never let critics define you. You get to decide who you are, and nobody else.

I still find it crazy to be recognized for *RHONY.* I was known in certain circles in New York before the show and would often see a lot of people from the fashion, art, and music worlds out and about. But today it's a very different scenario. I'm talking about strangers introducing themselves over a bin of avocadoes at Whole Foods. Generally when people approach me in person, they're very kind, and it's incredibly meaningful to me that anyone would take time out of their day to say hello or tell me about something I said or did that resonated with them. I've been surprised and touched by how many people have shared their own struggles with mental health and alcoholism and felt represented by my honesty on the show. It's moments like those that really make up for the shitty comments and tabloids, and reassure me that I'm in exactly the right place, doing exactly what I'm meant to be doing.

Improper Etiquette

Every one of my castmates is a deeper, more complex, and more interesting woman than I ever imagined. As much as they all love having fun and looking beautiful, there's more to them than meets the eye, and they each bring a wealth of experience to the table. These women are hustlers! I approached the show thinking, *What can I learn from these ladies?* The truth is, they have a lot of wisdom to share, even if they're not always intentional about sharing it. They've lived through some shit, and they have more years of life experience than I do. I'm grateful to each of them for the lessons they've taught me—whether they realize it or not.

Luann has taught me about the beauty of throwing a small, intimate dinner party, about creating an environment that facilitates ease. She has a very European flair for hosting, and a deep appreciation for conversation and a meaningful exchange, orchestrating magical moments in a beautiful setting.

From Ramona, I learned that you can look hot and have fun at any age.

Sonja taught me an incredibly valuable lesson about protecting my daughter. Since I was entering the public stage as Kiki was becoming a teenager, Sonja always hammered into me: It's all about Kiki and her privacy.

I think Sonja is a fiercely protective mother, and I respect the way she has separated her family from the show.

I count Tinsley as one of my very best friends. She has an amazing sense of humor, and when we're together, we spend the entire time laughing until we cry. She is truly drop-dead gorgeous, and yet she doesn't internalize that. She's a genuinely good, kind person. I mean it when I say there is not one competitive, jealous bone in this girl's body. That's inspiring just on its own. I want to be more like that.

I admire Eboni's confidence. She's an unapologetically ambitious woman, striving on her path to success. Just like the title of her book, she's *Pretty Powerful*.

Dorinda once told me that the benefits of being on the show won't last forever. She encouraged me to use the *RHONY* platform to my advantage while I have it. She reminded me that it's an incredible opportunity to build a brand, but to remember that it's fleeting. It's some of the shrewdest business advice I've ever received.

These women are also boss bitches. I've learned more about being a bitch from them than anyone else. They are assertive, hardheaded, loudmouthed, stubborn, controlling, and dominant. Yes, please! These are the qualities that have helped them achieve so much and provided them with the guts to redesign their lives and relationships at any stage of life. So much of the joy that fans and viewers get from watching any of the Real Housewives franchises is seeing women own their power. None of these women are wallflowers. None of them lack the confidence to ask for, or more likely demand, respect.

Today I've come to realize that reality TV is what you make it. It can be empowering if you make it empowering. It can be demeaning and belittling and even destructive if you let it take over your life. A lot of people say it's lowbrow TV, but let's not ignore the communities that have been built around Bravo and other reality shows. There are podcasts, social media communities, and a cottage industry of merch based on the Real Housewives franchises. In its own unique way, reality television has brought people together. It's escapism certainly, but through access to the inner lives of other people, viewers gain insight into struggles and relationships that might inspire them in their own lives. During COVID, when human interaction was almost completely stifled, reality TV provided some much-needed contact. My first season on *RHONY* aired just weeks after we went into lockdown, and I heard from so many viewers across the country who were grateful to be engaging with what felt like their besties. It's a safe space to relax and laugh along with your favorite Housewife, or Bachelorette contestant, or fashion designer.

It's possible to use the platform to your advantage if you don't let it swallow you up. I'm grateful to have had the opportunity to challenge myself and grow—even if that growth sometimes looked like, well, chaos.

CHAPTER 7
IT'S ALL CONNECTED

What do a lapsed Catholic, a Jew, and an alcoholic have in common? They are all parts of me—past, present, and future. Just don't let them walk into a bar. All of those challenges, wrong turns, and diversions were connected, and taught me who I am and what I really want in life.

I have zero doubt that everything in life is connected. All of the seemingly random events—your biggest challenges, your fiercest opponents, your happiest days, your darkest moments—all happen for a reason. If we could only see the underlying wisdom and logic in those so-called "mistakes"—the years spent partying too hard, dating fuck boys, or running from reality (as the case may be). As crazy as it seems, the wrong turns often lead us to the right place. It's a process that is iterative and ongoing. I'm a mother in progress, an entrepreneur in progress, a feminist in progress—a woman in progress.

One thing that is definitely part of my evolution is my spirituality. I am a born seeker, always looking for new ways to understand life and the universe and to feel connected to the world around me. Sometimes that happens when you take away the substances and booze. You look elsewhere for comfort, for a system or an order to hang on to. What keeps us from staying awake all night wondering about the meaning of life, why we're here, and why life can be so relentless? It's either alcohol or drugs, or food or sex . . . or sometimes spirituality. Maybe even all of the above. We need something to blunt the raw nerves that make it tough to be a feeling person *and* to live.

I've always been spiritual and had a relationship with G-d, even when I was at my lowest, most self-destructive period, and I've explored different belief systems and religions. I think I loved hallucinogens as a teen because when I came back down to earth, I felt like I had a bigger and better understanding of the interconnectedness of all beings. I've always asked myself questions like: What the hell am I doing here? What is the point of anything? My baseline is pretty nihilistic, so I need to put in extra work to find a more optimistic view and a higher purpose or connection in life. I'm also seeking an understanding of life and death, and although I still don't have the answers (and probably never will), the seeking itself is meaningful. I still ask myself if G-d is real every day. I have an abstract idea of what G-d is, but, for me, believing and connecting to a higher power is uplifting and life-affirming.

Faith has not only brought me comfort but also a sense of a higher order—a system outside of ours that connects us to itself and to one another. I'm currently in the process of converting to Judaism, which I've been working toward for two years. I feel a connection to Judaism that's different from anything I've explored in the past, and I'm immersing myself in it at a time when I really feel good in my skin. The very definition of faith is believing in something that you can't see or quantify, and taking such a leap is a tall order for a for cynic like me. It might be all bullshit. I truly hope there is a G-d, but I question it every day. Luckily Judaism, and the amazing rabbis I've been working with, have allowed me the space to keep questioning and exploring as I find my way on this journey.

Religion has been a part of my life since I can remember. I was raised in a Catholic family. My brother, sister, and I were all baptized in the same church in Chelsea where my dad and my grandmother Cele were baptized. We went to church some Sundays and on holidays, and

I went to Catholic school, of course, so religion was very much a part of our daily lives. I loved how beautiful the church was, and I even loved the smell of it. Those early years of being raised Catholic created a strong spiritual foundation for me. In high school, I still prayed and had a relationship with G-d, but we didn't go to church much as a family. I was praying to the rave G-ds at the time.

A Higher Consciousness

In my early thirties, I discovered a new way of viewing spirituality that sparked excitement and wonder in me. One of the most beautiful and affecting practices I studied was Bhakti yoga, better known as the Hare Krishna movement. Around 2014, I found my father's Bhagavad Gita (one of the sacred texts that is also a cornerstone of Hinduism), which the Hare Krishnas had given him in the '70s. I opened up the thick book with its ornate red cover and started to read. The Bhagavad Gita was written in Sanskrit, and its teachings are derived from ancient Hindu texts, which state that the Supreme Lord and humans are eternal spiritual beings trapped in a cycle of reincarnation. The way out of the cycle is through improving one's karma. I felt like I had found the answers to the fucking world.

One of the prominent messages of the Bhagavad Gita is: "The person whose mind is always free from attachment, who has subdued the mind and senses, and who is free from desires, attains the supreme perfection of freedom from Karma through renunciation." I mean, how happy would we all be if we could attain this state of consciousness!? I still read the Bhagavad Gita all the time. I keep it next to my bed.

I studied at a Hare Krishna temple, the Bhakti Center, on Second Street and Second Avenue in the city for years. I made my family and friends come with me from time to time—including my mom, Kier, and Rob. Rob and my friend Leslie would join me for weekend workshops where the monks held classes on the Enneagram, a really interesting way to decode the human psyche through its nine interconnected personality types. I went to Bhagavad Gita study groups, and one of the monks, Rasanath, became my spiritual coach. He would meet with me at my office, or bring me along to see his own guru speak. He helped to show me that the underlying message within the Bhagavad Gita is that your intention matters most—even when you're making mistakes or destructive choices. That idea really spoke to me. I got to the point in my studies where if I could have gone to India for a few months and immersed myself, I would have. Who knows how long I would have made it in a

Hare Krishna center in India, but I like to romanticize the idea.

Rasanath took me and several others from the Bhakti Center to see his guru to speak one day. As I listened to this man, I looked around and observed the entire auditorium sitting in rapture, hanging on to his every word. It was awe-inspiring to see him hold the attention of so many people . . . but also a bit intense. He took questions at the end, and someone asked, "What do I do about regrets that I have in my life?" The guru replied, "I know a man who is in Alcoholics Anonymous, and he told me that they don't have regrets. They just use their experiences to help someone else. So that's what you should do." *Holy shit!* I felt like that message was meant for me. The guru had told me to just keep working the program. The very act of continuing on—of sharing, of connecting, to say nothing of sponsoring someone—is about supporting and helping others.

That was one of the most profound lessons I learned from my time studying Hare Krishna, and maybe in my life. It helped me to make sense of my feelings of remorse and shame for the years of bad behavior, self-harm, and pain inflicted on those around me. It took years to work through, but that moment was the start. As years went by and life happened, I drifted away from the Bhakti

Center. But the experience remains in my heart, always. My years there undoubtedly made me a better person.

Embracing My Jewish Soul

I really think I have a Jewish soul. I could intellectualize why I'm converting, but it's honestly deeper than intellect. I have many Jewish friends, and as I've gotten older and helped them to celebrate Shabbat or attended their weddings, I've begun to ask more questions of them. Every question I ask is met with an answer that is both firm in its footing and able to be looked at and interpreted from many angles. I feel like so much of Jewishness is questioning things, and maybe that's why I like it. It's not a particular practice or belief. It's the sum total of viewing the world, life and death, and humanity in a way that feels connected to me. It's a soulful calling, not an intellectual one.

As I learned more about Judaism, my friends would sometimes say that I should convert, and what began as a throwaway musing became a calling inside me. I said it first as a joke, "Oh yes, I want to be one of the Chosen People," and then I began to say it in earnest. The truth is, I have a gut, emotional feeling that it's right. In fact, the Talmud, which is the primary source of Jewish law, describes someone who is converting as "a convert who comes to convert," rather than a gentile or non-Jew who comes to convert, a way of suggesting that converts have always had a Jewish soul.

Conversion to Judaism is a very strenuous process, and you have to be truly committed to do it. It can take a year or more to complete your studies with a rabbi, depending on if you're converting to Reform, Conservative, or Orthodox Judaism. There are weekly sessions with a rabbi to learn the basics of Jewish law and the tenets of the religion. It's taking me longer than a year at the moment, partly due to COVID and my schedule filming *RHONY*, and partly because I'm not rushing the process. I'm enjoying spending my time learning about Judaism and learning to speak Hebrew for prayers. You may remember the episode of *Sex and the City* when Charlotte converted, and she had to knock at the rabbi's door and ask three times before she was admitted to her studies. The same was true for me!

There are so many things about Judaism that appeal to me. I love the Jewish approach to mourning. The concept of shiva (the weeklong mourning period for first-degree relatives) is more relatable to me. How beautiful to sit for seven days and have people visit you. I also want to observe Jewish holidays. Right now I'm really enjoying the Friday-night tradition of lighting the Shabbat candles and observing Shabbat.

Shabbat is Judaism's day of rest on the seventh day of the week, in honor of G-d resting after creating the universe. It begins at sundown on Friday, and for the next twenty-four hours, observant Jews refrain from work and commerce; some don't drive their cars or use electricity. It's a beautiful idea to close out the week with such a pause and to refocus on family. The Jews I know embrace vastly different interpretations of Shabbat, ranging from taking complete breaks from technology to attending synagogue to sharing a lovely meal with family. I try to put my phone down, get off social media, turn off the TV, and focus on friends and family, disconnecting and resetting after the week. But I am not perfect at it, especially after thirty-eight years of not doing it. I already have Jewish guilt, obviously. One of my good friends who is Jewish told me that however I choose to observe Shabbat should make my life better, should enrich my spiritual practice, and not seem like a burden. So I'm just taking it week by week and doing what feels right as time goes on.

I believe that any spiritual practice or religious practice is *practice*—something you do over and over again to hone, like a skill. I know myself and the structure of organized religion is going to be what I struggle with the most. I'm sure I'll go to Shabbat services, but I also know that I won't always make it to every service. I want to observe Jewish holidays, but I'm not yet sure how observant I'll be, overall, on a daily basis. Just like with the twelve-step program—I've taken off months at a time, and even years, but it's always in my heart.

The final steps in the conversion process include a *mikvah*, the ritual bath that will symbolize my rebirth as a Jew. I will also be asked a version of this question: Do you agree to take on the Jewish faith despite persecution and discrimination? At a time when anti-Semitism is on the rise, this question feels more important than ever.

I'm converting to be a better person, and to be a happier person, more grounded, fulfilled. I want to have a strong and supportive sense of community, which is part of the reason that I'm drawn specifically to Judaism. And there is a structure to the Jewish practices and calendar that provides some order to my life. Ultimately, when I'm connected to a spiritual practice, I'm so much happier.

At the end of the day there are millions of people clinging to different religions and spiritual practices and belief systems, and no one can say for sure if any one of them is "right." My belief is that they're all right. As long as your spiritual practice helps you feel good and centered, and inspires you to live a better life, then that's all that really matters.

Just as my family has supported me in my spiritual endeavors, I support Kier in hers. My mom has been Kier's CCD teacher over the years, and I'm happy she took the reins and helped to give her granddaughter a strong spiritual foundation. Kier was recently confirmed in the Catholic Church, but I also want her to feel empowered to find a spiritual path that speaks to her. She's come with me to my Jewish conversion classes, and learned a little about the holidays and beliefs along the way. She's not against it, and I don't push it. Who knows? Maybe one day she'll want to explore Judaism, or head over to a lecture at the Bhakti Center.

Leaving a Legacy

Just because I'm converting doesn't mean I'm abandoning my past. I always found solace in religion, and that includes the Catholic Church for most of my life. When I first got sober in 2009, I felt like I was crawling out of my skin for most of that year. I sometimes found myself walking the streets, crying my eyes out, and not knowing what to do. And in those moments, I would quite often stop into churches all over the city. I would sit in a pew, in the middle of the sanctuary, and feel such comfort as I prayed for help, for strength, for clarity. When I didn't know where else to go, I went to church. I had long stopped taking communion, but I still felt connected. There was something about walking into a church that felt familiar. I loved the smell of the incense burning in the thurible that was swung around during mass, and even though I didn't believe much of what was being said at mass, I still found peace sitting and staring at the paintings of the saints, the Blessed Mother, and Jesus.

Being raised Catholic was more about culture to me and less about religion, so maybe it's not all that surprising that I stilled turned to it. My grandma Cele had crosses and statues of the Blessed Mother displayed proudly throughout her apartment. I am not one of those people who grew up with religion being forced down their throats. It never felt like that at all. My parents are not and were never fanatical. I was not traumatized by Catholic school, and while we went to church for holidays and some Sundays, it never felt like too much. To me, it felt like a tradition and a passing down of shared beliefs and beautiful rituals that connected us through the generations.

Family was always important to me even if I spent part of my life running away from mine. Just like I sought out the refuge of the church when I was struggling in new sobriety, I also sought support and comfort in the arms of my family, particularly my grandmother.

My dad's mom, my grandma Cele, took me in and let me live with her when I needed to get out of the halfway house. And my mom's mom, Grandma Marie, was my staunchest supporter. I remember getting a call from her out of the blue when Kiki was about six years old. She said, "If no one has told you they are proud of you, I am." I'm not sure she knew how much that phone call meant to me, but I will never forget it. She was the one person in my life who made me feel like I wasn't a fuckup. She always praised my business savvy, my co-parenting skills, and my sobriety, and her approval was everything to me. She was the matriarch of our large Irish-Italian family and raised eight kids, with fourteen grandkids— she knew a thing or two about comforting people. My Grandma Marie was the person I feared disappointing the most. Maybe the only person.

It's difficult to imagine someone so vibrant and so important falling ill, but in the summer of 2020, that's exactly what happened. Grandma Marie was diagnosed with colon cancer, and her decline was swift and devastating. I knew we weren't going to have her forever, but still, I struggled to wrap my head around the thought of her not being with us one day. I went to visit her in the hospital when COVID protocols prohibited more than one visitor at a time. In some ways, that limitation was a blessing. We were the only people in the room for one of our last conversations, a memory I'll always cherish. She validated me in so many ways, sharing her insightful observations and sage wisdom for the last time. She acknowledged some big things for me, including about my breakup with Rob, that I had been yearning to hear. She helped to set me free from so much guilt.

As I was sitting with her in her hospital room, a pair of social workers entered to discuss hospice care with her. I didn't think that I should be the person to help her through such a conversation, so I started frantically texting my aunt and mom to join us. I really didn't want to watch her confront her mortality and the reality of the situation. But the social workers started talking to her, so I took a deep breath and held her hand. She squeezed mine and I squeezed hers back. She told them she didn't want to go home to die. She wanted to fight. They explained that going home just meant she would be more comfortable. So we took her home and made her comfortable, and enjoyed the time we had left.

There was something heartbreakingly beautiful about watching and being a part of my grandmother's process. We all piled into her room one day with a nun and prayed and listened to a song that my grandmother loved. Maybe she was scared, but she didn't show us. She stayed strong while we all took turns weeping and clinging on to her. She asked that every Sunday, we gather at her house. She would come downstairs and sit outside for as long as she could as we all talked and laughed and cried together. I have no idea where she found the strength, but she did. She commanded so much respect and integrity, even as she faced the end of her life. I know she wasn't ready to die, and even though she lived a full life of eighty-eight years, it still feels like she was taken from us far too soon.

Until the end, Grandma Marie continued to impart wisdom, and I was hit hard by how fleeting and precious life is. My mother told me my grandmother never thought about dying. She was too focused on living. When my time comes, I hope I can face death with the strength my grandmother did. I want to die knowing I lived every moment to the max. I want to die with no regrets and nothing left undone. I want to die with the knowledge that I said *yes* to the call to adventure when it came, that I apologized for being an asshole when it was due, and that I spent as much time as possible with my loved ones.

Forget Regret or Life Is Yours to Miss

While I will always acknowledge the mistakes I've made, I don't really buy into the idea of dwelling in regret.

Even the most difficult, shameful, damaging moments of my life have taught me something and helped me evolve. When you're focused on what happened in the past, you're not spending your precious energy on your present and your future. I think it's important to accept the moments you fucked up, make amends to anyone you might have hurt, and then make amends to yourself.

I've struggled for so long with the effects of feeling powerless over my life that I have to make a conscious effort to stay focused on what I *can* control. When I started to work on myself and realized that my expulsion from school set me on a destructive trajectory—drinking, doing drugs, disappearing, hurting my family and myself—I felt an urge to beat up on teenage Leah for not being better and doing better. But now when I think about that thirteen-year-old girl, still really a kid trying to both fit into an intense environment and find herself as a young woman, I feel compassion. She was doing her best and didn't have the tools to do better. Back then, I felt like I had no autonomy and no choices. By numbing myself with drugs and alcohol, I was running from the pain and the fear, which snowballed as my regrets grew; and by putting myself in dangerous situations, I was proving to everyone else how little I valued myself. I was immature, lost, and unable to be gentle, to forgive, or to understand what I really needed. How can I be mad at a young woman who was in so much pain?

When I got sober and started working the twelve-step program, I learned a lot about accountability. I dreaded the infamous step of making amends to people whom I've harmed with my addiction, but through my work in the program, I finally understood the importance of owning your behavior and being able to meaningfully apologize.

My parents were pretty high up on the list for my apology tour after the years of disappearing and drug-addled screaming (and also for the time the drug dealer showed up at their doorstep with a gun). Now that I'm the parent of a teenage girl, I recognize the impact my behavior had on them, and I fully acknowledge that I put them through hell. But I knew I couldn't wallow in the ways I wished things had been different, or that I had been different; I could only apologize for the pain I caused and move forward.

I decided to talk to my parents separately to honor our individual relationships, and it was very powerful to have such an intentional moment with each of them. On a beautiful summer day, I drove up to Connecticut to see my parents at the home that I once felt was a prison, to say the things I should have said years ago. They weren't used to me having such a vulnerable moment with them, so they were a little taken aback. But they knew I was working the steps, and that I would be making my amends at some point.

I started with my mom, taking her into the living room and sitting next to her on the coach. Then I went outside to talk to my dad, who was mowing the lawn. He turned off the mower and we talked under one of the big trees out back. The conversation was very similar with both of them. I told them that I was sorry for all of the devastation, the sleepless nights, and the chaos I had put them through. They both had very similar responses. With such compassion, they told me there was no need to apologize and that it broke their hearts that I had to bear the alcoholism gene that my mother, also sober, had hoped would skip a generation. That was a pivotal point in my relationship with my parents. I felt that, for the first time ever, they acknowledged how much I had suffered because of my addiction and my mental health struggles. I felt validated. I felt loved. I felt forgiven.

Until that moment, I didn't know if they recognized that I was struggling at the hands of a powerful disease. I felt that they attributed a lot of my behavior and substance abuse to being irresponsible or making poor decisions—like it was a moral failure. I'm not shirking my responsibility here; I made choices, obviously, but I really felt like they weren't choices at the time. I was so beholden to my addiction, and the associated self-destruction, that it became my identity; everything else kind of disappeared. The deep, feverish urge to have a drink or get high was overpowering and I felt helpless in its grip. When I wanted to get lost from myself, the itch began, and I would follow it, no matter where it led me and no matter who I hurt along the way. It felt more like a need than a choice.

I also apologized to Rob for what I put him through. It breaks my heart when I think about the chaos I brought into our young family as I struggled with alcoholism and new motherhood. Rob isn't a big talker, so it wasn't a long conversation, but he was appreciative that I acknowledged my behavior and apologized formally.

Next, I called Rob's mom. I told her I was in the program and asked if we could talk. For years, Rob's mother and I had a very strained relationship. It was your classic significant other/mother power struggle, and it felt like we were in total fucking competition over everything from the moment Kier was born (she actually made baby announcements without telling me, using a photo I didn't like, and then sent them out to everyone we knew). Petty stuff aside, though, the real issue between us was that I always felt like she resented me, that she thought I wasn't good enough for her son. Over the years, we had little fights over minor issues. They were never real arguments with yelling, just constant passive-agressive exchanges.

I drove to her home in Connecticut and, sitting across from her, I apologized for my behavior. I took responsibility for the tension between us, and I felt a weight lifted. I'm grateful we had that opportunity to talk things through, because not long after we spoke, she was diagnosed with cancer and passed away within months. Had I not apologized to her when I did, we might never have had the chance to find peace in our relationship.

It's powerful to humble yourself to someone. As I learned about the Jewish holiday of Yom Kippur during my conversion, the idea of an annual ritual of atoning really resonated with me. During Yom Kippur we ask G-d for forgiveness for our transgressions against others as well as forgive those who have transgressed against us. It's actually not so different from the process of making amends in twelve-step programs. Holding on to resentment and grudges only hurts you. I've learned that doing the work to heal from the past is necessary for a better future. Forgiveness is freeing.

Sometimes forgiving yourself is the hardest part of atonement, but it's essential. Holding on to shame and regret prohibits growth. I love the idea of a yearly reset;

of starting over with a clean slate, letting go of the guilt, and allowing others to do the same.

Perfect Doesn't Exist

Kier has a great saying: "Perfect doesn't exist." The perfect life, the perfect relationship, the perfect body, the perfect mother, the perfect job—none of it is real. I take a lot of comfort in this thought, and when I can let go of the drive to be perfect in anything I do, I can focus on the overwhelming good and beauty there instead. It's hard for me not to criticize myself and pick apart what I'm doing wrong—especially as a mother—but at the end of the day I'm doing the best I can. And that's really all any of us can do.

For me, a fear of failure is at the root of my strive for perfection. I think this is pretty common—most of us are afraid of failing or embarrassing ourselves. But if you let it, that fear will stand in the way of trying new things that might just be the biggest and best things you've ever done.

I spent too long running from the chaos in my life, from the uncomfortable feelings that I didn't know how to handle. I wish I could have appreciated then how much each decision, each impulse—each flap of my wings—mattered. I wish someone had told me what I've since learned: That my choices and experiences and relationships and even my pain were all interconnected in one complicated, messy, beautiful web of existence.

CHAPTER 8
F*CK
GRAVITY

When people ask me why I have to do things the hard way, I always say, "Because I have to do it *my* way." My path may not be the easiest, but it's the authentic one for me. Through the failures and hardships, the triumphs and defeats, I've learned so much about who I am and how I see the world. If mistakes are our greatest teachers, I've been under the tutelage of a pretty amazing faculty.

We live in a society that likes to point fingers at others instead of encouraging honest dialogue and introspection. That kind of grace to learn from a mistake is one rarely afforded by the quick-to-judge hordes on social media. An angry mob taking down their target is a powerful force, but our ability to see the nuance in situations and not condemn all who disagree must rise above. We've established how interconnected we all are, and I'd like to see people take the time to have tough conversations instead of tearing one another down. There is so much wisdom to be gleaned when we open ourselves up to the ideas and opinions of others. Imagine how we would all grow if we stopped shutting down conversations and started looking for opportunities to learn, and helped others to do the same.

Don't think I'm not taking my own advice. I'm working to become less judgmental and more aware of my own biases. We all experience the world through the unique lens of our individual lived experience, which includes all of the facets of our identity, obviously, but I hope we can also start to focus on our shared humanity. As a society we have become divided in so many ways, and it seems like everything is analyzed through a political and polemic lens. It's lifelong work, but I'm on it, working to decipher my thought processes and worldview. I believe cultivating compassion and self-awareness is the biggest tool we have toward creating real change, to making laws that help to create a better future for everyone—and challenging the ones that threaten it.

Free Your Mind and the Rest Will Follow

In this climate of public reckoning, so many of us are walking on eggshells, terrified to make a mistake that will get us called out. As a culture, we've become *so* quick to tear one another down, to point out discrepancies, uncertainties, and mistakes along with true bigotry, purposeful ignorance, and hatred. It is nearly impossible to seek truth through an exchange of ideas. But I refuse to live in fear. I refuse to live my life worrying about who I will offend by speaking my mind. I've always called it like I see it, and when push comes to shove, speaking my truth outweighs my fear of being canceled.

"Cancel culture" is the most overhyped phenomenon to come out of the last couple of years, and I think we need to reflect on what it's doing to us. It's a losing game for everyone. Cancel culture is a one-size-fits-all approach to our nuanced world. Making mistakes and learning from them is supposed to be part of life. When did we decide that anyone who has ever fucked up deserves to be publicly shamed? I feel badly for young people who can't learn their lessons without an angry mob waiting to condemn them.

Cancel culture is damaging for progress. We're avoiding

important conversations, and we're missing important voices and points of view because we're bullying or ignoring those we don't agree with. In the end, this disconnection is hurting us all. Let's challenge the rules that limit our capacity for growth and change.

Social media has stunted our natural way of relating to and processing our fellow human beings. If you make a mistake, you're canceled. If you change your mind, you're a hypocrite. Fight that binary world. There is so much more than right or wrong. It's hard, but it's worth it to live a life of possibility, complexity, and reinvention.

If you're a human being, you have most likely held two differing opinions, believed in something your actions didn't support, or done things that conflict with your conscious beliefs. I'm never going to apologize for being a human being. Can we please normalize changing our minds, learning new things, and evolving? We should always seek new information and different opinions so that we can learn other perspectives and fact-check and gut-check our own. And if, in that process, we change our minds—that's okay, too! My views have changed a lot over the years. I said things in articles and interviews when I was twenty-four that are different from how I feel today. That's why I hate the whole idea of punishing people for past mistakes. When did we become so unforgiving? When did we become so puritanical? If we continue to hold people to this standard, then we're all going to cancel ourselves.

The thing about cancel culture that really pisses me off is how much pleasure the angry mob takes in calling someone out. I'll acknowledge that some people genuinely believe they're doing the right thing by pointing out an error in speech or perspective, but we've all seen the righteous joy of online crowds as they take someone down. I'm not trying to join the angry mob; I'm trying to unpack the difference in opinions, and I'd like to see more people take the time to correct and educate others, instead of tearing them limb from limb.

I'm all for changing your mind as you learn and grow and gain new perspective, but it's important to also *know* your mind. When faced with pushback or criticism, it's easy to second-guess yourself. One of the hardest skills to master is knowing your mind and being able to articulate your beliefs. People will try to label you because it's easier to think in cut-and-dry terms even though humans are complex (or at least we should be). There will be haters and naysayers no matter what you do, so you might as well do what you want. Too often, we bite our tongues to avoid upsetting people or pissing them off. I still catch myself holding back my opinion occasionally, but a whole lot less often than I used to. It's nice to be liked, but it's better to be honest.

When I began using the word "bitch" as an empowering term and part of MTTM's slogan, I wanted to reclaim it for myself and remind women everywhere to own it. If I live in my truth and people don't like me because of that, I can deal with it. I would rather voice an unpopular opinion and be hated for it than be loved and accepted based on a lie.

Don't Fuck with a Feminist

I've always considered myself a feminist, even as the waves of feminism come and go and the pendulum swings back and forth. It's a term I can't—and won't—give up. I bask in my femininity. Pussy Power for life! That said, feminism is not a one-size-fits-all term. No one person can speak for all of feminism, or for all of womankind throughout the world. It's belittling to women to even pretend that what we're all fighting for is the same.

I'm so tired of performative activism and feminism where women fill their social media feeds with "feminist" posts, quotes, reading lists, and photos of marches, who act outraged about issues they know so little about because they think it's "cool." I see those celebrities who put on their pink pussy hats and march, who wear the little pins onstage as they name-check feminist icons.

I call bullshit. Those are the same people doing movies and signing deals with rapists, taking money from
corporations who have no female executives, or worse.
People talk so much about the best way to use their
"platform," but I think it's more important to take action in real life than to post it on your Instagram, don't
you? Real change comes from within, not from wearing
a "Feminist AF" T-shirt.

I think people love to see women fighting with one
another. Women don't need men to create competition
among them. Rivalry among women is bred from a lack
of power as we've internalized patriarchal messages.
Women mistreat, compete, and distance themselves from
other women in order to increase their power and standing among men. That mentality is a result of condition-
ing, and we've got to rise above it. Take, for example, the
pop culture polls that compare famous women. You know
what I'm talking about—the articles and clickbait conversations such as: Who wore it best? Who looks younger,
fitter, sexier? Which Housewife would you rather hang
out with? I'm a competitive person, but I'm not competitive with other women. I'm doing me in my own lane,
working toward my own personal goals.

The Real Housewives franchise sometimes comes
under fire for being anti-feminist, but it's probably the
most feminist endeavor I've ever been a part of. It's a real

platform for women of a certain age, in an industry that often devalues them. As women get older, there are fewer parts for us in Hollywood, fewer opportunities offered in business, and less tolerance of our sexuality in society. Whereas men apparently become silver foxes in middle age, women contend with the reality of biological shifts and physical changes that are seen by many as an expiration date. For a woman to age gracefully, she's supposed to invest in a wardrobe of beige cashmere and work on her Bundt cake recipe. The ladies of *The Real Housewives* are throwing a dirty martini in the face of that idea!

I think it's absolutely refreshing and inspiring to see the women of Real Housewives living their dreams in middle age and beyond. Seeing the women embrace their sexuality; talk about seeking pleasure; and sharing experiences, needs, and desires on national television feels so empowering to me, and I think the reception to their candor is encouraging. Viewers are seeing that their sexuality can be celebrated without a limit on age, preference, or experimentation. They haven't lost touch with that part of themselves, and I hope they never do. You are never too old to reinvent yourself, to find love, to start a new career, to be confident, or to just have fun.

The Real Housewives shows are also about female

friendships in their raw forms—which is sometimes ugly but always honest. Female friendships are celebrated and cherished; opinions are staunchly defended. Women raise their voices and hold their own. In fact, most women on the show are neither wives nor housewives, and have taken the show in a different direction, showing brash, strong-willed *friends* navigating midlife.

The problem is—if I can summarize a century of feminist debates and acts in about one sentence, which I probably can't, but watch me try anyway—is that women want equality. Fuck equality. Why aren't woman stepping into power? The only way to dismantle a system that has so long favored men is to swing the pendulum in the other direction—hard. So-called feminists should take a break from retweeting and crocheting next year's hats and start running for office, jumping at every opportunity for corporate advancement, making their art/music/movies/clothing as boldly as possible and—radical as this may seem—supporting one another along the way.

Wear the Damn Pants

Fashion and feminism have long been intertwined, as men have often controlled how women dress and present themselves as one of their tools of oppression. That's why the idea of burning our bras was a powerful visual used by the feminist movement of the 1970s. Even the idea of wearing pants was once controversial! And now we have another extreme of women posting provocative, nearly nude photos of themselves and calling themselves feminists and reclaiming the word "slut." I'm all for nudity and being a slut—just take a look at my Instagram! But not everything has to be a feminist statement. Sometimes a thirst trap pic is just a thirst trap pic. You can admit that you want to look sexy without defending it as part of a larger ideology.

The world of streetwear has always been a toxic place for women. Sometimes it seems like it's only getting worse. I remember being in the back of my friend's shop in 2003, when Supreme released their calendar. It was being passed around, and the crew of guys were ogling it. When it finally got handed to me, I saw an image that was so disturbing it's stayed with me to this day: an extreme close-up of a woman's vagina and backside, spread wide open. Her finger was shoved deep inside of her vagina, and only a ring with the word "Supreme" spelled out in diamonds was peeking out. I am (clearly) not shy about sex, sexuality, nudity, or anything of that nature, but I was stunned. It reeked of misogyny, of the idea that women are little more than something to fuck.

Without a doubt, we have to take some responsibility for the pressure put on women, in terms of our image and our appearance. So much of the need to dress and look a certain way comes from wanting to impress or compete with other women. Women dress for other women so much more than they dress for men, sometimes without even realizing it. Do you think your boyfriend is going to compliment you on your Bottega Veneta bag or your new pair of Roger Vivier sandals? Let me tell you right now, he won't. A guy would probably like to see a hot woman in a white tank top. When women dress for one another, you see the designer labels and the complicated styling that only other women would notice. In theory, that's great—except that too often women tear each other down instead of building each other up. There's nothing wrong with *everyone* looking good.

Sex Positive

On my last season of *RHONY*, my tagline was, "I'm sex positive and BS negative." A lot of people have asked me what I meant by that. The best way I can explain my interpretation of sex positivity is that I believe in creating the space to enjoy, explore, and learn about sex and sexuality without judgment or shame. It's not about promiscuity, orgies, swapping partners, or free love. It's about owning what you want in your sex life—whatever that may be—without fear of ridicule or judgment. It's about removing the embarrassment around knowing your own body and advocating for your own pleasure.

There are too few sex educators out there teaching women how to have good, pleasurable sex, and, as a result, women are ashamed to ask for it. I'm no Dr. Ruth. Being sex positive is easier said than done. Most of us grow up with hang-ups around sex. After all, sex is a messy part of human nature. We're surrounded by mixed messages from our parents, the media, pop stars, and religious institutions. Women are told that our value is based on how few sex partners we have, but at the same time, how fuckable we look. We are sexually objectified in every single fashion ad and movie, but we're also told not to be "easy." It's so confusing. That's why I decided that I'm going to do whatever I want when it comes to how I look and who I fuck. Sometimes that means going a year without sex. Sometimes it means having multiple partners in one week. Sometimes I want to leave the house looking like a sex kitten. Sometimes I wear Birkenstocks and sweats. At the end of the day, it's all about what makes me feel good.

What other people think has no bearing on how I

view my sexuality and my sex life. If it did, I would be married or in a committed relationship right now. But I'm more interested in living my life and working on myself than in outside pressures, compromising, and settling. In some ways, I'm still figuring out what I want in a relationship. I consider myself mostly "straight," but I have been attracted to women in the past.

My first sexual experience was with women. In ninth grade, I had some beautiful moments of exploration with two friends in the city. A few of us took acid and sampled liquor we found at my friends' apartment. Later that evening, I had a threesome with two other girls. It just happened organically, with us taking a bath. I'm sure the booze and drugs helped move it along. But truthfully, I just felt more comfortable with women at that point in my life. This wasn't my only experience with women over the years, but it helped me understand that sexuality is a spectrum. Thankfully, our culture no longer views sexuality as strictly binary.

I have a lot less sex than I used to because there are just fewer people who I have chemistry with. I find sex without chemistry to be like coffee without caffeine. What's the point? Sex is an exchange of energy, and I'm not willing to trade any of my energy for mediocre sex with some random dude. I need to have trust, a friendship, and a rapport with someone to have good sex. I'm not looking to waste my time having bad sex.

My views on my own sexuality have changed over the years—from sex while high to sober sex, from too much sex to hardly any sex, from men to women, and couples. I remain open to seeing what happens. They say that women hit their sexual prime in their forties, so I think I'll know sooner than later. But for now I like experimenting with different looks more than I like experimenting with different dicks.

This Is Your Brain on Sex

I'm fortunate, in many ways, to have grown up in the '90s during a time in pop culture when women were breaking barriers, rejecting stereotypes, and embracing provocation. That was especially true in music. When I was a teenager, I watched Madonna's music videos over and over again on MTV, particularly "Like a Prayer," in which she burned crosses and kissed a Black saint. It was so scandalous at the time of its release, in 1989.

I came of age with a few key icons who, to me, embodied the kind of power, confidence, and ownership of one's sexuality that I longed to embrace, no one more than Lil' Kim. I have always loved hip-hop, but so much of it was demeaning toward women. Let's just be real: a lot of lyrics were about sexualizing and degrading women, treating women as less than. Lil' Kim came on the scene and was flipping it on the guys. Her lyrics portrayed a strong woman in charge of the situation. She acknowledged that women were being called "hos" in other lyrics, and she embraced and redefined it to be a good thing. Her lyrics were about taking that power back, like, "Okay, call me a ho. I'm gonna fuck you, and then take all your money, or make you buy me a Chanel bag or car or house." Lil' Kim acknowledged that sex was about more than pleasure; it was about power. And she was giving it back to the women. When her debut album, *Hard Core*, came out in 1996, it was exactly the call to arms we all needed to hear. She encouraged women to demand their fair share—of the spotlight, of fame and money, and of pleasure in the bedroom.

In a way, she fought the hip-hop patriarchy like a feminist queen. Through her lyrics, she opened up to her fans about what she'd experienced and how she found the strength, wisdom, and guts to live through it all. Life mimics art, and that was the beginning of a lot of women owning their sexuality and using it to get what they want. Instead of playing the innocent card, she was revealing and sexy on her own terms.

To me, Cardi B is this generation's Lil' Kim. I thought

her performance on *SNL* while pregnant and wearing what looked like a wedding dress was incredibly powerful. She's an ultimate sex symbol who is outrageously unapologetic about her sexuality. Her lyrics and music videos make conservative pundits who are normally free-speech advocates blow their lids like the Evangelicals of the '90s. And here she is showing her baby bump to the world publicly for the first time while singing her hit "Be Careful" and holding her belly. We can be overtly sexual and still get to have our vulnerable, soft side as well. We get to have a range of feelings and emotions, and we don't need to apologize or explain it to anyone. When censorship is at an all-time high, I celebrate freedom of speech and the right to enjoy sensuality and sexuality. I admire any woman who is using her body in the way that she wants. I think it's terrible that OnlyFans has threatened to forbid explicit videos on their platform. OnlyFans is a subscription-based social network similar to Instagram in its photo and video-forward content, but consumers pay to see the posts and to engage with someone. It's a safe way for women to make money from explicit videos and photos, and some people depend on it for their livelihoods. Women who are supporting themselves this way are at the mercy of the company, which can decide at any moment that explicit material is banned. Doing so would drive these women to less safe scenarios. Sex work is never going to stop. So why not make it safe? OnlyFans holds all the cards and can change the policy again down the road. Women, everyone really, should have autonomy over their own bodies and be able to make their own choices about what to do with them.

Look, I know that a porn is problematic—there is so much out there that is degrading and demeaning to women. A lot of porn is based on the idea of men taking control, objectifying women, and focusing solely on their own pleasure. I'm not advocating for porn that teaches men that women want to be choked, take it in the face, or get banged in the ass (unless that's your thing). But I still strongly believe that sex work—whether it's pornography, prostitution, or anything else—should be made safe and legal.

Raising a Daughter

Parenting a daughter has been one of the most instructive experiences for me in fully understanding womanhood. The ways I feel about my own femininity, sexuality, body image, and place in the world have shifted as I've encouraged and advised Kier over the years. Motherhood is as ugly as it is beautiful, as exhausting as it is life-affirming. It's like having a live mirror that shows you your every strength and flaw, if you're brave enough to look. Kier makes me grateful in a way that I wouldn't be without her. She lets me love in a way I could never love without her. She is my greatest teacher and challenger.

Being a mother has been so important to my growth as an individual. Now, at fourteen, Kier is growing up and becoming a young woman. When I look at her, I'm reminded of my struggles at her age, dealing with the pressures, the bullying, and the quiet work of teenagers trying to figure out who they are and where they belong. It's hard to navigate the path of becoming your own person while dealing with social pressures and the critical gaze of other women—and, too often, the sexually charged gaze of men.

As the mother of a teenage daughter, I think about slut shaming a lot. My instinct is to protect Kier from the criticism and judgment of other people and, of course, the sexual attention of men. It's a very difficult line to walk. I want Kier to dress age appropriately and not provocatively, but I also understand the desire to have fun and be able to express yourself. I work hard to make sure

I'm not accidentally making my daughter feel ashamed of her body or the way she chooses to dress. I don't want to make her feel bad, ever, but Rob and I have to protect her, even if it means pointing out the ways she might be vulnerable. A few times, she's gone shopping without me and bought more revealing articles of clothing that I wasn't aware of. I've had to delicately navigate how to tell her what she shouldn't wear without damaging her self-esteem. I want her to be confident and empowered, but also safe and realistic in our fucked-up world.

The first time Kier posted on Instagram, I was half proud of her and half terrified. It was a series of three photos taken while we were in Miami, and I found them to be really inappropriate. One of the images was just a picture of her from waist to neck, so it felt like it was about her body, and not about her. I talked to Rob, and he agreed. We explained to her that when you put something on the internet, it stays there forever—and she may not want these pictures floating around one day.

I wanted to make sure she didn't feel ashamed about it. I understand wanting to feel sexy, and even be provocative. I get all of that. Hell, I'm the same way! I told her that she looked great, but that she has plenty of years to post images like that and to feel that way; it just wasn't the time right now. She wasn't happy, but ultimately she deleted the post. I know that she's living in a more en-lightened world than I was growing up, but that doesn't mean there isn't judgment. I'm so glad I'm raising her in New York, where she'll meet all kinds of people and, I hope, be accepted for exactly who she is.

As a young girl living in Chelsea, I always felt free to express myself in any way I wanted. After we left the city, I was surprised to be criticized for the way I dressed. Slut shaming can come in the form of being teased and ridiculed for the way you dress, the way you talk, or for your actual sexual activity. Sometimes it can even just be about the way you look. I experienced some of these forms of hostility when we moved to Con-necticut.

I'll never forget my first experience of being slut shamed. I was hanging out at my house with girls who I thought were my friends. One of them left a notebook behind, and when I opened it, I found nasty notes about me, including a drawing of me in the peacoat I wore to school every day, my legs spread open. The caption next to it said: "I bet Leah wants to sit spread eagle in her peacoat and she's not wearing anything under it." It's laughable to read now (can you imagine a less sexy item of clothing than a peacoat?), but at the time, it really hurt. I dressed differently from most of the other kids in my high school. I had a more flamboyant style that was often a little more provocative. I would wear some midriff-bearing tops or miniskirts, which sometimes stood out compared to their J. Crew catalog looks. Still, having a different personal style doesn't give anyone the right to pass judgment. Sure, I had a boyfriend, but I was much more interested in doing drugs and getting fucked-up than getting fucked. I confronted the girl who wrote it, and when I did, she felt stupid. I realized that it ultimately said more about her than it did about me.

I believe that it's important to be honest with Kier about my experiences as a teenager. She asks me about *everything*, and I pretty much give her straight answers. Sometimes I don't know if that's right or wrong, but I feel like the best way to prepare her for being a woman in this world is just to have as much information as possible. When she asked me what an AA meeting was, I told her. I explained that I used to drink too much and that the meetings and the program help me not to drink. I've told her that not drinking is a struggle for me, and that she might be genetically predisposed to having the same struggle. I talked to her about a lot of my experiences as an adolescent and teenager. I told her that addiction took over my life, and took over our whole family. I want her to understand the consequences of her actions as she starts to navigate the rough terrain ahead. Being a teenage girl is not for the weak.

Own Your Upgrades

At age thirty-eight, I found myself getting plastic surgery for the first time. Maybe I finally did it because I was surrounded by people who have all gone under the knife, or maybe it was because plastic surgery is as normal as going for an annual Pap at this point, but for the first time it seemed like something I could actually do. The thought of going under anesthesia had always terrified me; I had never had any type of surgery before getting my nose job. It just all seemed so foreign, until one day . . . it didn't. I guess staring at yourself in high definition can do that to a person! In September 2020, I walked right into that plastic surgeon's office on Park Avenue and never looked back.

It really didn't come as a surprise that my mother was disappointed. She had put it in my head from a young age that I should be happy with what G-d gave me, even though I had always changed up my hair color. I never took my appearance too seriously, and I had fun experimenting with different looks. There was just one part about my nose that I'd long wanted to fix, and finally, I had the means and the opportunity to get it done. So I did! Why wouldn't I? The result is so subtle that my mom asked me why I did it. The answer is that I wanted to look like myself; I wanted to look natural while fixing what I perceived to be a slight flaw.

That's something that I wish I had known when I was younger: that you can love yourself, and still improve or change yourself. Those two things can coexist. You can do whatever the fuck you want! My experience with plastic surgery has been positive, but I can see where it may get complicated. The problem arises if you're trying to fix something that goes *beyond* the physical—if the plastic surgery is a placeholder for a deeper unhappiness and dissatisfaction, if it's not really about your nose, or boobs, or whatever else.

I had such a great experience that a couple of months after my nose job, I went back to the same doctor for a breast lift and implants. I decided to get my boobs done over the holidays in 2020, taking full advantage of the COVID quarantine to recover. I'd always loved my boobs, but after breastfeeding Kiki for fifteen months, they changed. I wanted an upgrade. I wanted Leah-circa-2006 boobs.

I'm very happy with the results, but I'm also very glad that I waited until now to do it. I felt mature enough to make this kind of decision with eyes wide open. I'm actually looking forward to my next procedure, which I'm sure will be my eyes. I just wish celebs would be more honest about the work they've had done. It isn't fair to make people think that aging isn't affecting them when in fact they are spending hundreds of thousands on work. Talk about unrealistic expectations of beauty!

I never thought about hiding my plastic surgery from the tabloids or the world. To me, that would indicate that I'm ashamed of having the work done, which couldn't be further from the truth. I posted pictures of my black eyes after the nose job, and my recovery after the boob job. I owned it all. Why should I feel bad about doing exactly what I want to do? Why should anyone else get to decide what's accepted and what's taboo for you and your life?

I make no apologies about investing in my appearance. At this stage in my life, I've spent a lot of years investing in my insides, doing the truly hard work of battling my demons and trying to be a better person, and now I want my exterior to reflect the progress I've made. After all, you can be the prettiest bitch in the world, but if your heart and soul are ugly, well, no surgery can fix that.

CHAPTER 9
THE TAROT CAN'T TELL YOU EVERYTHING

(but bitch, I love a séance)

If there's one thing I can tell you with absolute certainty, it's that the future is impossible to predict. And yet we spend so much time trying to do just that. We read our horoscopes, visit psychics, or, in my case, have my cards read by Barbara Corcoran. But even the best psychics/mediums/real estate titans can offer only an educated guess about what's around the corner. I mean, if the last few years have shown us anything, it's that the future is frustratingly unknowable. For anyone with anxiety, that thought might keep you up at night or lead you to drink it away.

We can't know what tomorrow will bring. And as much as we try to do just that, we still beat ourselves up for what we didn't see coming. Things rarely go according to "plan" (but that *is* the plan!). So where does that leave us mere mortals? All we can do is show up and embrace the unexpected.

These days, the Category 1 hurricane has been downgraded to more of a tropical storm. I've found some balance in living the wild, adrenaline-filled life of my dreams while keeping my feet on the ground enough to stay sane and healthy. All those years of snorting, chugging, and disappearing taught me that the beast inside me was going to require more than ecstasy, weed, and alcohol to be tamed. A conventional life was never going to cut it for me—it just wouldn't be enough. I needed to figure out how to satisfy my pull toward living on the edge in a different way—a way that wouldn't end up with me in a gutter, or a jail, or worse. It's not about choosing good over bad; it's about prioritizing my well-being.

Real growth starts when you're tired of your own bullshit. It takes a lot of strength and resilience to recognize what's not working for you and make a change. I've learned how hard it can be to even admit that something needs to change, but believe me, it's worth it. Just like in the program, admitting you have a problem is the first step. I've always been unapologetic for who I am as a person, but that doesn't mean I'm not introspective or that I don't hold myself accountable for times I've fucked up or hurt someone. I have to work at self-care, at my sobriety, at my relationships. It's a daily commitment to be the best person I can be for myself, and show up for my daughter, my friends and family, and all of the people who count on me.

Train the Tiger

One of the people who has been instrumental in helping me find healthier ways to cope with my demons is my boxing trainer, Martin Snow. I'd walked by his gym in Tribeca, Trinity Boxing Club, a million times, but when I got sober in 2009, I finally decided to stop in and see what it was all about. I had so much anxiety and adrenaline coursing through my veins as I detoxed from booze . . . I knew I needed a rigorous exercise routine to serve as an outlet. Boxing seemed like the perfect way to get out some aggression and help my body find balance.

When I first walked into his gym, Martin said he could feel that I was different from the "average blonde" who stops by the gym to tone up. To this day, I don't know if he actually felt that way or if he's just a great bullshitter, but I'll believe him for the sake of the story. Martin is full of unusual wisdom, and when we work out together, he often shares pieces of advice and encouragement that really speak to me. He knows about my background, my hang-ups, and my struggles. Early on in my training he told me, "Everybody has a tiger inside and you have two options—tame it or train it. Most people try to tame it. Give it alcohol, drugs, junk food, or whatever will keep it sedated, because G-d forbid it gets loose. Then everyone is dead. The problem is, tigers eat meat, and if you're feeding it that other stuff, then *you* are on the menu. The second option is what we do: train the tiger. Put it through its workout, then feed it a piece of meat. Now walk down the block with a tiger on a leash and tell me how you feel: invincible. That tiger was your best friend in the world until somebody told you it wasn't."

The tiger is your power. It's the fuel to your fire, your passion, your creativity, your ambition. These are the things that make you . . . *you*. As crazy as it may sound to get into this level of philosophical musing while sweating my ass off in a boxing gym, it was exactly what I needed. As I learned how to box, I learned to respect my tiger.

There's something in all of us that's a little wild, a little dark, and a little scary. When you discover how to tame your beast, you can do anything.

We Are Who We Are

I've spent a long time thinking about why people are the way we are. Why are some people addicts and alcoholics, while others can snort a few lines without making a mess of their lives? Why do some people fall in love and stay married for fifty years, and others move from relationship to relationship, never quite satisfied? Why do some people find contentment sitting quietly on a park bench, while others jump out of airplanes searching for adventure and distraction? Maybe some of it can be chalked up to fate or random luck. Maybe it's nature and nurture. Certainly, some of it has to do with the inherent inequities built into the very fabric of our culture and economy. But also . . . maybe I'm focused on the wrong question.

Maybe the only thing that really matters is what kind of life you live, even when the odds are stacked against you. Especially when the odds are stacked against you. Undoubtedly, some people have better options to choose from than others, but just about everyone has the ability to fight and punch their way into being a better version of themselves.

People struggling with mental health issues or addiction and alcoholism reach out to me all of the time to share their stories or ask for guidance. I'm not a professional, obviously, but I've been through so much that I do have some advice. While there are no magic answers, and everyone's battle is unique, the one thing I do know is that most of the time, you can't help anyone who suffers from addiction if they don't want to be helped. People have to ask for help in order for any type of intervention to be meaningful. People who have an addict in their lives can only offer love and support, opportunities, and chances for that person to change and redeem themselves. I don't know that I totally agree with the tough-love approach that some programs espouse, but again, it's a different journey for everyone.

I wish we had better science on the nature of addiction and alcoholism. I would love to understand why some people are able to get clean and sober—and maintain that sobriety for years—while others constantly struggle and relapse. I used to have a theory that some people were just in too much pain—that getting clean and sober would mean dealing with the pain, and it was too much of a burden to bear. And while I acknowledge the role of spirituality in recovery, it's hard for me to attribute getting sober to divine intervention. Why would G-d help one person and not another?

Addiction is so much bigger than what you *should* or *shouldn't* do. For me it comes from a dark place, from something broken inside me that I'm only just learning how to fix. I've spent the last thirty-nine years trying to calm the storm raging inside me. Over that time, I've often wondered what kind of voids I must be trying to fill with substances. I've come to realize the answer is both simpler and infinitely more difficult than pinpointing my "issues": At my core, I'm someone who really likes to get fucked-up. It's not all about long-term resentments and damage. It's also about the chaos of my emotions matching the chaos of my actions. When I achieve that kind of equilibrium, I feel a sense of peace—even as I'm sloppy, screaming, or getting naked and throwing tiki torches on television. I like to skip out on reality, but I've got to rein it in to live the fully realized life of my dreams.

At its core, substance abuse is a form of coping. We all have different coping mechanisms to help us deal with our raw nerves and the unfair twists and turns that life brings. Some people go for a run, call a friend, meditate, or throw themselves into their work. Other people binge eat, watch porn, gamble, or have random sex. My coping mechanism was once drinking myself into oblivion and huffing poppers on West Fourth Street. We're all looking for something to blunt the force of reality, to soften the sharp edges of life. There's nothing wrong with coping mechanisms, unless they're slowly killing you.

For me, and for many others, addiction is a need at the cellular level that make us unable to control ourselves. I experience it as a need that turns off all critical thought and all ability to put healthy limits on my behavior. It's made me lie and cheat and steal and abuse and torture myself and the people I love. The only way out is to own your powerlessness—and through that paradox, you can gain some control. I've found it so empowering to own who I am, addictions and flaws, strength and beauty. When you stop running from yourself, you can start to love yourself.

I'm striving to use healthier coping mechanisms to deal with my anxiety, and the sadness and the uncertainty that still live inside me. I'm not a fortune-teller, and I make no promises for the future. But that's not the choice I'm making today. I'm choosing to love myself and to focus on better, healthier habits for me—and for my daughter.

Get the Fuck
out of Your Way

This book isn't my victory lap. It isn't a celebration of all that I've done and accomplished, though I am proud of so much. It's a record of all of the ways I took the hardest road to becoming myself.

I've been running Married to the Mob for more than fifteen years, and over that time, I've been the toast of the town and nearly out of business. I've had collaborations with top brands and seen my designs on celebrities in the tabloids and on red carpets, and I've made mistakes, launched products that didn't sell, and made business deals I would come to regret. I've had a lot to learn, and I've learned it.

Owning who you are and being comfortable in your skin are the most difficult and most important skills to learn. I am not a natural businesswoman, and that's something I had to work at over the years. I've always had the creative vision and excelled at sales, but I've struggled with running the supply chain and balancing the books, among other things. It was something that bothered me for a while, but I've finally realized there is no shame in knowing what you're not good at. I've sought out people to teach me and help guide that end of my business.

Being real about where you're at and what you're thinking is *healthy*. I've seen plenty of entrepreneurs, artists, and musicians get caught up in the machine of projecting success. They don't hone their skills, or know who they are and what they stand for because they're pretending to have achieved a level of success or notoriety they're not ready for. I do buy into the "fake it till you make it" mentality, up to a point. But the most successful people I know have given up the pretenses and owned their journey each step of the way, including embracing their failures and the lessons they bring. They're humble and they've put in the work, so when they achieve their goals or reach a level of fame, they're ready for it.

With years of public scrutiny under my belt, I know that I would be absolutely lost if I didn't have a strong sense of self. When the tabloids, fans, or social media trolls are calling you beautiful and ugly, a bully or a victim, a style icon or a hot mess, you don't know what to think unless you already know who you are. If I allowed the changing tides to affect my sense of self, I would really be struggling. But instead, I'm standing strong (most of the time).

These days, I turn to people I trust when I start getting down on myself. I acknowledge the self-doubt and nagging self-criticism without letting it swallow me up, and I remind myself that it won't matter in a week. I try to keep things in perspective, to catch the negative thoughts in their infancy, and to speak over them with strength and positivity. I accept that I'm an introverted extrovert, so I take the time by myself to decompress before throwing myself back into the world.

It's easy to look around and compare yourself to others, especially on social media. Instagram is a fantasy; we all know that. And yet, I think competition has its benefits. No one likes to lose, and often that drives better performance and improvement. It's a lie to pretend that I'm above the comparison and competition game, but I know how important it is to stay focused on my own goals and not chase someone else's version of success. The race is long and, in the end, it's only with yourself.

I don't think that any of us have as much control over our lives as we think we do. In the letting go of control, I find my freedom. I've come to accept that the unknown is the key to creativity. When we let go of trying to wrestle our lives into the perfect vision of what we think they should be, we can begin to build the life we want. I can decide how to grow my business, how to expand in my career, how to love whomever I choose, and how to be whatever version of myself I want to be.

Feeling Yourself

Dealing with addiction and mental health issues can be a full-time job. I'm still learning to live with the noise inside my head, and some days are better than others. Sometimes I maintain a routine that serves me and helps me to find peace, and other times I'm a wrecking ball looking for something to tear down. If I start feeling like shit, I know what to do: I call my shrink; I go to the gym; I talk to my close friends. There are periods of time that I drop into my body and live without the demons chasing me, and I'm always grateful for them. Thankfully, those moments are becoming more and more my norm.

I'm also paying more attention to the basic stuff that keeps my body regulated and my soul balanced. Exercise releases the feel-good hormones and endorphins I desperately need, so I throw myself into workouts like I once dove onto an open bar. These days, I'm enjoying boxing, running, and even figure skating—all activities that steady my nerves. If I'm in a bad place mentally, I know that I can change how I'm feeling by leaning on one of these activities. I try to eat a healthy, balanced diet 80 percent of the time and get a solid eight hours of sleep at night. I hang with people who add to my life instead of ones who detract from it. I make time to be alone and recharge.

Let's not get carried away. I'm not perfect, and I certainly don't make the healthiest choice every time. But I try to consider the options available to me when I feel that familiar itch start to spread. And I'm working on not losing it when I get off track for a few days or a few weeks. Extremism is extremism, whether it's alcohol or exercise. So I practice moderation—pizza when I want it, and workouts when I'm feeling it. It's not an all-or-nothing game.

Most addicts are impulsive. There's such a short amount of time between my thought and my action. I'm working so hard to create more space between my impulses and my actions. It's emotional maturity—finally, at age thirty-nine. I'm getting better at pausing and thinking before doing, which opens up choices that I hadn't considered before.

Maintaining my sobriety and my mental health is a constant part of my life. Even though I feel great now, it's not as though addiction is something that exists in the past; it's very much at my doorstep. When the pandemic hit in March 2020, just a few weeks before my first season of *RHONY* aired, I decided to stop drinking. I hope that I won't drink again, but I also know that I need to take my sobriety one day at a time. Right now, I don't drink. I smoke weed occasionally—which some call "Cali-sober." It's not the right choice for everybody, but it works for some.

Sometimes when I'm feeling anxious or struggling with depression, I turn to my mom for her advice and perspective. My relationship with her has evolved so much, and she's become one of my most important sources of support and wisdom. She reminds me that I'm not going to feel great all the time, and that not every day has to be a good day. It may sound simple, but it's an important reminder when I get into a state of having high expectations or putting pressure on myself to be a certain way. The same pressure and energy that has helped me achieve all that I've achieved also trips me up and creates a sense of doom and disappointment when things aren't amazing. So with her help, I've been able to snap out of feeling sorry for myself when things aren't going perfectly. We're not entitled to good days every day. That's dangerously unrealistic.

Although I try to stay focused on the present, I have started to set some goals for myself. Don't get it twisted; I'm still me. I don't have a five-year plan, and I'm not making a fucking vision board. But I do have a clearer sense of my priorities and what I want to spend my energy on. I want to spend more time with my family. I want to see more of the world. I want to own who I am and continue to find peace in my life. I want to savor every moment that I have.

Finding Meaning
in the Madness

Sometimes the best things aren't those we ever intended to happen. I've learned by now never to say never to anything, to answer yes to adventure when it comes calling. I have accomplished everything in my life out of sheer luck, hard work, and circumstances. I've never had a long-held plan or adhered to long-term goals. The path to where I am now has been circuitous at times, but I couldn't have landed here if I hadn't listened to my gut and said yes to new opportunities. I would never have believed that I would be on a Bravo reality show, or that I would be living through a global pandemic *and* writing a book. Strange things can happen when you jump into the unknown. That's where the magic is.

For so long I told myself a story about my life, that I fucked things up and did things the wrong way. Now I know it's not true. The events of my life unfolded just as they should have. The chaos brought me opportunities and pushed me to find my own way. It turns out, there *is* a method to my mess. I'm not the girl of my youth, acting out of pain and anger. I'm not the young mother unsteady in her new role. I'm not the inexperienced entrepreneur struggling to keep a business afloat. I am so much more than I had been giving myself credit for, and it's time I acknowledged that.

I can't end my story without also acknowledging one of the most important, unsung characters in my life: New York City. The city is a part of my DNA, my blood and bones. It's the energy that courses through my body and the creativity that lights up my brain. It's been my support system and my destruction, seeing me through my brightest days and my darkest hours. Together, we have risen from heavy blows and continued to thrive.

I've experienced some of the city's toughest moments right along with her: September 11, Hurricane Sandy, and, of course, the COVID-19 pandemic, which took so many beautiful lives in this city and jeopardized the very fabric of New York. Living in this city during the height of lockdown, feeling the heaviness of collective loss and grief, reminded me that there's no time to waste in this life. It's true that we can't predict the future—the pandemic was probably one of the most unexpected events in all our lives. I want to be fearless. I want to live knowing that I can cope with whatever comes my way.

Writing this book has been its own journey in self-discovery and awareness. I've begun to own my story in ways I never imagined. When I started writing, I shied away from calling myself an entrepreneur or believing that I had anything worthwhile to say. It wasn't humility, believe me. It was true self-doubt and discomfort that surprised even me. I feel so confident in so many ways, and I act as if I have it all figured out. But much of the time I have imposter syndrome. For so long, I viewed myself as a teenage delinquent who got lucky. But when I relived my journey in writing this book, I saw how much I had actually accomplished and felt like I deserved it. In reliving my teenage experiences, I see that I've been holding on to those emotions: feelings of rejection, being less than, and not belonging. I've felt like a fuckup for most of my life, and I've never truly let go of feeling small and unworthy. Writing this book has allowed me to feel proud of myself for the first time.

There is so much power in the stories we tell ourselves about ourselves. That narrative had been controlling me and holding me back until I began to write my own story. It was only through the writing process— which, it turns out, is 90 percent reflection and 10 percent writing—that I began to see myself for who I am: flawed, dynamic, creative, strong, and, yes . . . chaotic.

ACKNOWLEDGMENTS

To my Married to the Mob family, my Supreme bitches, and to the streetwear community who has loved me, supported me, and inspired me throughout the years—thank you. You have been my mentors and friends, and my constant North Stars along the way. Rest in peace, Keith Hufnagel and Virgil Abloh.

To Andy Cohen, Bravo, and Shed Media: Thank you for giving a downtown girl a second shot on the Upper East Side. I've loved my time on *RHONY*, and I will always treasure the incredible memories.

To my friends, co-conspirators, and badass icons: Cat Marnell, for your encouragement and eagle eye. Camille Paglia, Diana Gerich, Robin Walker, Leslie Cross, Lourdes Castro, Tinsley Mortimer, Peter and Jackie Bici, Nancy Rommelman, Mish Barber-Way, Kathy Iandoli, Eric Helgas, Laura Stylez, Rita Linkner, Alejandra Hernandez, Sherry Kosovic, Fafi, Todd and Dana James, Kelly Cutrone, Mitch Fisher, and Jordan Littlejohn—thank you all.

ACKNOWLEDGMENTS

To my glam team, the real heroes of the story: Colby Smith, Netty Jordan, and Kory Fitzpatrick.

Thank you to my editor, Julie Will, for pushing me to write this book and to own my story. Your vision and guidance throughout the process were everything. And to Emma Kupor for all of your help. Thank you to everyone at HarperCollins for believing in this book.

Jen Schuster, thank you for your guidance and helping me to see my journey in new ways.

Thank you to Eve Attermann and Bradley Singer at WME, and to Gary Adelman, for always having my back.

To my wonderful, kooky, loving family: Dad, you are the big mac! Sarah and Danny, it's an honor to be your sister. My sweet niece Cecilia. My badass aunts Vicky, Pam, Chris, Maria, and Pat. The entire Castellano and Savona families. My grandmothers Cecilia and Marie—I miss you so much.

Rob Cristofaro, thank you for letting me be me and for loving me all the while.

My beautiful, precious daughter, Kier—I love you. You've taught me more about love and life than you'll ever know.

ABOUT THE AUTHOR

LEAH McSWEENEY is a streetwear pioneer, entrepreneur, cultural provocateur, and founder of Married to the Mob, one of the first streetwear brands for women, by women. Since launching her brand in 2004, she has brokered exclusive partnerships with MCM, Kangol, Barbie, Paris's Colette, Reebok, and Nike. Following the incredible success of Married to the Mob, in 2020 Leah launched Happy Place, a luxury sleepwear line. She is a frequent contributor to *Penthouse* magazine, Hypebae, and Mass Appeal. She joined *The Real Housewives of New York City* in 2019 and continues to advocate for female empowerment, street culture, and creative entrepreneurship both on- and off-screen. Leah lives in New York City with her fourteen-year-old daughter, Kier.